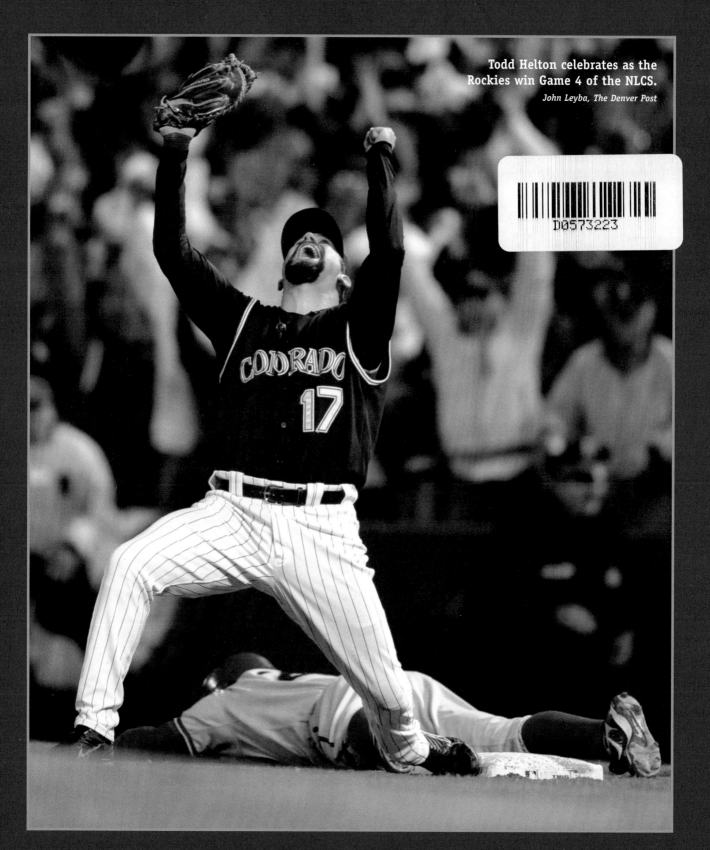

Todd Helton celebrates as the Rockies win Game 4 of the NLCS.
John Leyba, The Denver Post

D0573223

TRIUMPH
B O O K S

Manager Clint Hurdle celebrates with Kazuo Matsui on the field after Game 4 of the NLCS. *Andy Cross, The Denver Post*

Published by Triumph Books, Chicago.

All stories and photos © The Denver Post except where noted otherwise.

Editor: Scott Monserud
Photo Editors: Mark Osler, Tim Rasmussen, John Sunderland, Ken Lyons and Craig Walker
Copy Editor: Greg Henry
Library Research: Barry Osborne
Cover photo by John Leyba.

Content packaged by Mojo Media, Inc.
Editor: Joe Funk
Creative Director: Jason Hinman

This book is available in quantity at special discounts for your group or organization.
For further information, contact:

Triumph Books
542 South Dearborn Street
Suite 750
Chicago, IL 60605

Phone: (312) 939-3330
Fax: (312) 663-3557

Printed in the United States of America

Brothers Joseph, right, and Jacob Coolbaugh, ages 5 and 3, respectively, throw out the ceremonial first pitch before the start of Game 3 of the NLDS. Clint Hurdle revealed the team voted a full playoff share to Amanda Coolbaugh, whose husband, Mike Coolbaugh, was killed when hit by a foul ball while coaching first base for the Rockies' Double-A Tulsa squad on July 22. *Helen Richardson, The Denver Post*

CONTENTS

A Great Way To Grow 6
World Series 8
NLCS 24
NLDS 42
Wild-Card Playoff Game 54
Worthy of an Encore 58
The Streak 62
Power of 64 68
Spring Training 76
Yankees Sweep 82
Player Profiles 86
Woody Paige 120
Stats 124

A GREAT WAY TO GROW

When the Rockies made their World Series debut in Boston, their mostly homegrown roster displayed an unmistakable bond

By Troy E. Renck

October 24, 2007

Before they faced The Green Monster, they shared green chili burritos. Before they faced the Boston Red Sox in the World Series, they learned how to clean socks in cramped Laundromats. Before they walked onto the sport's ultimate stage, they ran up phone bills from remote minor-league outposts.

The Rockies made it to the World Series, an improbable opponent for the American League bullies. Aside from "Who the heck are these guys?" the most common question is how did they get there?

Statistics provide a healthy slice of the explanation. The Rockies won 90 games, won 21 of their last 22 overall prior to the Series. They featured an NL MVP candidate (Matt Holliday), a Rookie of the Year front-runner (Troy Tulowitzki) and everybody's sentimental favorite (Todd Helton).

Ultimately, the team of Destiny collided with Broomsday, the Rockies swept in four games in the World Series.

To understand how the Rockies reached the sport's biggest stage, and found themselves on Yawkey Way in October, you must get closer. You must walk into their clubhouse. Of the 25 players that made up their World Series roster, 15 were raised on the farm. They weren't just home grown, they grew up before each other's eyes.

The Rockies are that unique pro sports franchise that discovered success through friendship and unmistakable camaraderie.

"Anytime you spend so much time together and get know each other families, there's going to be a stronger bond," explained Holliday, the first of the minor leaguers to breakout during the 2004 season.

"We have been together for years and it's been great because all of the new guys have fit in well, too. I don't think you necessarily have to have this to win, but makes it easier and a lot more fun."

The Rockies finished last in the National League West last season. They were close then, too, right? So what happened? Their bond grew tighter through failure, when they failed to meet expectations in the second half of 2006. And they became better players.

"We were mad we hadn't done well," outfielder Brad Hawpe said. "We knew we should be a good team."

Linear growth isn't common at the major league level, but it made sense to this group. They arrived in spring training this year with inflated confidence, their optimism akin to a college team with a strong senior class.

"I think through their education and their experience, they have really embraced each other's talents. They know that everybody out there has something to bring. They have earned their place, they have talent and they can help this club win," manager Clint Hurdle said. "I think that is the other unique characteristic. They are committed to doing whatever is asked of them to help the team win."

It doesn't hurt that they like each other. On the Sunday night before departing for Boston for the biggest road trip of their lives, nearly a dozen Rockies' attended the Broncos-Steelers' game at Invesco Field. During the season, the players held weekly barbecues or bowling nights. Ryan Spilborghs served as a tour guide for a field trip along the Freedom Trail when the team was in Boston in June.

"We're not just teammates. We are friends," Holliday said. "These are people we genuinely care about."

The bond was formed, for many of them, during late night bus rides through small towns, eating greasy potato chips, beef jerky, and the convenience-store delicacy: the burrito. They shared hotel rooms, commiserated over position changes, dissected their swings over swigs of soda pops.

"It was a close group, where guys were pulling for each other," recalled former Rockie Jason Jennings, who paid Holliday $100 a month to sleep on an air mattress in his Asheville, N.C., apartment in the minor leagues. "You are probably never tighter with guys than you are in college. That was what it was like, even when we were in the big leagues. The music was playing, guys were always talking."

Ripping is more like it. This team's affection can be seen in its endless ragging. Nobody is immune. They razz Tulowitzki over his encyclopedic knowledge of his own hits - there is a running counter above his locker, dating to his days in Little League. They presented a faux Purple Heart to Jason Hirsh after he pitched with a broken leg, stage Stupid Human Trick contests, with Josh Fogg the most recent target when, in two swings, he couldn't hit a

ball into the seats at Chase Field during the National League Championship Series.

Reliever LaTroy Hawkins credits Helton for making the vibe work. His comfort level has grown with the young players. He's become more accessible, the barbs now a two-way street.

"Now if you say something, it's not 'Holy (heck), I just made fun of Todd Helton I am going to be excommunicated," Sullivan said. "Or be designated for assignment."

In 2004, when most of the players came up, like Garret Atkins, Jeff Francis, Hawpe and Holliday, this dynamic didn't exist. The clubhouse was littered with mercenary veterans, who knew they were leaving or were threatened by the kids. When a few players replaced Francis' nameplate with "Franchise," Hurdle ordered it removed.

"They do things now that maybe they would wonder how I was going to react. Or what other people were going to think. Now they know it's all good," Hurdle said. "I trust them, they trust me."

In many ways, the Rockies' 1-9 June road trip typified how Colorado got here. All momentum from sweeping the Yankees had vanished, the season was on tilt. But rather than splinter or point fingers, the Rockies' bond grew stronger. It's why the World Series sweep, too many, is the beginning, not the ending of a great story.

"It's hard to comprehend what has happened this last month to get here. It's all gone by so fast. I can't wait to watch all on video after this is over," Hawpe said. "I am not surprised that we made it his far. I thought we were really good all year, one of the better teams. And we always believed in each other. ... To lose hurts. Now we want to get back here." ◼

GAME 1: At Fenway Park, Boston
Red Sox 13, Rockies 1

Inning	1	2	3	4	5	6	7	8	9	runs	hits	errors
Colorado	0	1	0	0	0	0	0	0	0	1	6	0
Boston	3	1	0	2	7	0	0	0	x	13	17	0

MONSTROSITY

Red Sox pulverize Rockies in Game 1 of the World Series
By Troy E. Renck

October 25, 2007

Even before Jeff Francis threw his first pitch Wednesday night, the Rockies weren't having a good day. Todd Helton required four takes to read the lineup for the Fox telecast. An annoying rain arrived soon after the national anthem. Troy Tulowitzki's name was misspelled on his new bats, with an s instead of z.

After the first inning, you half expected the Rockies to schedule a hastily called press conference to explain that everything was going smoothly. In fact, they were the target of an external malicious attack, the Boston Red Sox pummeling the Rockies 13-1 in the World Series opener at Fenway Park.

Can they get a ticket to hide?

"Obviously we have to change our game plan," said Helton, "because that was a beating we got."

It created an emotion inconceivable just a few hours earlier: sympathy. The Rockies waited 15 years for this, and they couldn't wait to get it over with. It began with a painful first inning, Francis tagged for three runs on five hits.

The first batter he faced, Dustin Pedroia, clubbed a home run. It wasn't a swing, it was an omen.

"It wasn't the layoff. I felt strong. I just made too many mistakes," said Francis, whose Rockies will attempt to become only the second team in 11 years to win the World Series after dropping the opener.

"There are no excuses."

By the fifth inning, it had gone past embarrassment to something more gruesome. Even Red Sox fan Stephen King couldn't bear to watch, spotted reading a copy of *Newsweek* magazine. Boston scored seven runs in the fifth and abruptly halted every meaningful Rockies statistic from the past six weeks.

Their 10-game winning streak, including their seven-game playoff perfection – over. Their 10-game road winning streak, dating to Sept. 13 at Philadelphia – done. Their feeling of invincibility – poof.

Despite their insistence that inactivity would not be a factor, the eight-day layoff left them stale, and out of sync. The Rockies appeared to be swinging their bats through maple syrup vats, unable to catch up to Josh Beckett's fastball.

"He's always been known since he was a young phenom and now he's living up to all the expectations," first baseman Kevin Youkilis said. "He's the guy we want out there in the big game."

If the Rockies were to win this game, they had to follow a specific game plan. Francis needed to change speeds effectively, and establish his fastball on the inner half of the plate to keep the Red Sox sluggers from reacting with ferocity to four-seam fastballs away. He immediately veered from the script and couldn't put away hitters with two strikes.

After 25 pitches, pitching coach Bob Apodaca vis-

Kazuo Matsui strikes out in the first inning in Game 1 of the World Series. *Glenn Asakawa, The Denver Post*

Yorvit Torrealba misses the tag on Kevin Youkilis, who scores during Game 1. *John Leyba, The Denver Post*

ited the mound, trying to soothe the pain.

There wasn't enough aspirin for this. The Rockies had allowed only 16 runs in the first seven games of the postseason. Their bullpen had surrendered just five earned runs. Franklin Morales, pitching in relief for the first time in his career, allowed seven in the fifth inning, retiring only two hitters. At least he got someone out. Ryan Speier was summoned to clean up the 21-year-old's bases-loaded mess and walked all three batters he faced.

"When you have a team plan like ours, it's kind of fun to watch," Beckett said. "You hear people say all the time, not too many pitchers last six innings against us."

Amid a purple haze of walks, balks and mistakes, Beckett was everything the Rockies were not. If openers set trends, the Rockies are in store for a lot of swagger and bravado from the Red Sox ace.

Beckett worked seven innings, allowing the Rockies'

only run on a Tulowitzki double scoring Garrett Atkins in the second inning. It wasn't so much what he did as how he did it. He didn't throw a breaking ball until his 18th pitch of the game, not unleashing a heater lower than 93 mph.

"His fastball had sideways movement," said right fielder Brad Hawpe, the fourth non-pitcher to go 0-for-4 with four Ks in a World Series game. "He was really good, give him credit."

For the Rockies, a glass half-full team, they left with one comforting thought – Wednesday's mauling counts only as single blemish, their recovery starting tonight with rookie pitcher Ubaldo Jimenez.

"This is not going to bother us as much as everyone thinks," Francis said. "We will come back strong." ■

Jeff Francis in the fourth inning, with the score already 6-1 Boston. *Andy Cross, The Denver Post*

GAME 2: At Fenway Park, Boston
Red Sox 2, Rockies 1

Inning	1	2	3	4	5	6	7	8	9	runs	hits	errors
Colorado	1	0	0	0	0	0	0	0	0	1	5	0
Boston	0	0	0	1	1	0	0	0	x	2	6	1

0-FOR-FENWAY

Colorado's once-mighty offense becomes swing and a myth

By Troy E. Renck

October 26, 2007

Two games. Two runs. No chance. It's as simple as that. Let MIT crunch the numbers, throw on a turtleneck and philosophize if you wish, but it really comes down to this: The Rockies haven't hit enough to win a game in May, let alone the World Series.

As euphoric as the past six weeks have been, the two nights in Boston were a sobering experience for the Rockies. Baseball hosted its biggest feast and Colorado's bats turned into linguini.

The final score in Game 2 on Thursday night at Fenway Park: Red Sox 2, Rockies 1. Translation: Green Monster, red faces.

"You can be frustrated all you want, but the bottom line is we need to do more offensively," slugger Matt Holliday said. "We haven't been able to string anything together."

In a game where they needed to make statement, the Rockies, down 2-0 in the Series, find themselves in a chilling predicament. For all intents and purposes, the Rockies must win out at Coors Field to have a chance to take this series.

Bats, not rings, are the glaring focus now. The Rockies are hitting .229 in nine postseason games. It makes what happened in the first two games feel less aberration and more like an accurate barometer. Against the Arizona Diamondbacks in the National League Championship Series, the Rockies delivered

the timely hit.

Now, as the Series shifts to Denver this weekend and Boston will lose its DH, the Rockies are struggling to make contact.

Of the 54 outs against the Red Sox, a staggering 22 have been strikeouts. This isn't supposed to happen in an American League park. Teams are supposed to let their hair down, and run around bases as if doing laps. The Rockies were running lapses.

"We seem a little too anxious," first baseman Todd Helton said.

"We are a team that generally puts the ball in play and makes the pitcher work, and we didn't do any of that here."

Two players illustrated the teams' divergent paths: Red Sox reliever Hideki Okajima and the Rockies' Ryan Spilborghs. Okajima made history, becoming the first Japanese-born pitcher to appear in the World Series. Then he made the Rockies look like relics, striking out four in 2 1/3 innings. Okajima, who made a winner of Curt Schilling, has not allowed a run in the playoffs in six appearances.

By comparison, Spilborghs served as the Rockies' DH and fanned three times. All looking. It was an indelible image on a night of missed opportunities and mental mistakes that were absent during the team's stunning 21-of-22 stretch.

Red Sox third baseman Mike Lowell deked Rockies

Julio Lugo hops over Brad Hawpe to complete a double play to end the second inning. *Andy Cross, The Denver Post*

right fielder Brad Hawpe in the fourth inning. Lowell casually rounded second on J.D. Drew's single. Hawpe squared up on the ball, rather than charging, and Lowell took off for third, sliding in safely just before the throw.

He scored on Jason Varitek's sacrifice fly. In the eighth inning, Matt Holliday recorded his fourth hit – the rest of the team went 1-for-25 - nearly sawing off closer Jonathan Papelbon at the knees. Before even throwing a pitch to Helton, Papelbon picked off Holliday.

"It was a simple throw, really," Papelbon said. "But it will probably go down as one of the biggest outs in my career."

The past two nights have been a series of cringes. This was a game to show they belong. But they seemed if not out of place, then out of sync.

Before the game, Rockies general manager Dan O'Dowd talked about the need to show swagger, pitch inside, punch back offensively. He was pumped

Matt Holliday is picked off trying to get back to first base by Kevin Youkilis in the eighth inning.

up, sounding like he was ready to take a bat to the plate himself. (Hard to blame him for being a little riled after Red Sox fans wore him out in the stands the past two nights.)

Ubaldo Jimenez revealed a sneer, pitching inside. He put Kevin Youkilis on his back. (You think it was an accident that the first pitch that Josh Beckett threw to Matt Holliday buzzed his chest?) Problem was, Jimenez blurred the line between effectively wild and just plain wild. He was gone after Lowell's fifth-inning double that put Boston ahead 2-1.

Helton produced the Rockies' lone run on a first-inning groundout, scoring Willy Taveras from third base. But what didn't occur became more significant. Too many strikeouts, too many outs, their results as empty as Fenway Park as their bus trudged toward the airport. ■

Ryan Spilborghs reacts after striking out for the third out in the top of the seventh inning. *John Leyba, The Denver Post*

GAME 3: At Coors Field, Denver
Red Sox 10, Rockies 5

Inning	1	2	3	4	5	6	7	8	9	runs	hits	errors
Boston	0	0	6	0	0	0	0	3	1	10	15	1
Colorado	0	0	0	0	0	2	3	0	0	5	11	0

BARELY THERE

Colorado rallies to within a run, but the Red Sox answer to near their second title in four years
By Troy E. Renck

October 28, 2007

Miracles don't have patents, but they do come with expiration dates.

The end hasn't arrived for the Rockies, but you can see it from here. It looks like a blank stare, grinding teeth and dented batting helmets. It looks like an American League pitcher driving home two runs with his first-ever hit. It looks like Rocktober is about to become Rocksover.

A team that produced the greatest finishing kick ever appears out of gas, its perfect ending out of grasp. It's hard to draw any other conclusion after the Boston Red Sox thumped the Rockies 10-5 Saturday night at Coors Field in Game 3, leaving Boston on the doorstep of its second World Series title in four years.

The Rockies have spent the past five weeks mocking history, doing the unthinkable. But to win their first championship, they would have to make history, becoming the only team to come back from a three-love Series deficit. Of the 22 clubs that have taken control in this fashion, 19 delivered sweeps.

"That's a good team. They have superstars up and down the lineup," reliever Matt Herges said. "You don't want to be in this position. It's do-or-die. But we have been in this situation before when we made the playoffs."

What stings is that the Rockies have had opportunities to make this a competitive series. But their offense didn't awaken until it was too late, too many taps on the snooze button. And setup man Brian Fuentes - so dominant until the final game of the NLCS - siphoned hope after the bats showed life, Boston tagging him for three runs in the eighth inning.

"Even when we get back in the game, they are hard to keep down," shortstop Troy Tulowitzki said. "We haven't been able to do it, obviously."

The Rockies haven't lost as many as four straight games since June 29. The Red Sox have provided a compelling argument that it will happen again after scoring 10 or more runs for the fifth time this postseason.

Because these are the Rockies, they made it interesting, entertaining the sellout, towel-waving crowd with a nervy comeback worthy of the first-ever World Series game in Colorado.

Matt Holliday, a strong National League MVP candidate, smoked a three-run home run in the seventh inning. The laser came off Red Sox reliever Hideki Okajima, a first-pitch, 83-mph changeup disappearing over the center-field fence.

In that instance, everything seemed plausible again. Holliday flipped his bat, knowing the ball was gone.

Yorvit Torrealba reacts to grounding out for the third out in the seventh inning. *Andy Cross, The Denver Post*

When he crossed the plate, the all-star nearly severed Garrett Atkins' hand, slapping five.

For a second, the swagger of the 21-1 stretch was back. Just as quickly, it vanished when Atkins and Brad Hawpe struck out, and then Yorvit Torrealba grounded out on Okajima's 29th pitch. The Rockies averaged nearly 10 strikeouts per game, buzzkill for almost every rally.

Drama was required because of another flawed performance by a starting pitcher. Josh Fogg, who has forged a reputation for slaying big-name opponents, shrunk in the spotlight. The Red Sox bareknuckled the right-hander for six runs and 10 hits in 2 2/3 innings, an outing Fogg called "awful" that was tainted by Daisuke Matsuzaka's two-RBI single.

When the third inning mercifully concluded, the Rockies seemed woefully miscast for the sport's biggest stage.

At that point, they had been outscored 21-2 and outhit 33-12, appearing as nothing more than a stutter in the Red Sox's acceptance speech.

While the lineup absorbed blame for the Game 2 loss, the rotation has been a disappointment, especially when comparing its previous postseason work. In sweeps of the Phillies and Diamondbacks, the starters produced a 2.43 ERA. Against the Red Sox, that number has ballooned to 10.81, with Jeff Francis, Ubaldo Jimenez and Fogg all failing to work at least five innings.

"They have been great for us all year," Holliday said. "I think it's our fault for putting too much pres-

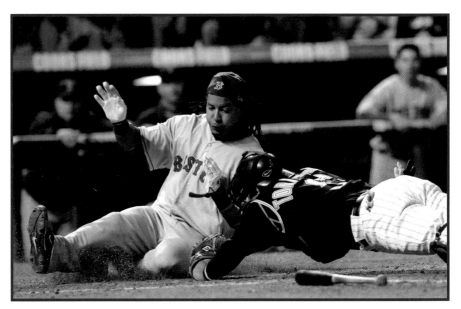

Yorvit Torrealba tags out Manny Ramirez in the third inning. *Andy Cross, The Denver Post*

sure on them by not getting leads."

After 23 mostly forgettable innings, the Rockies finally fought back in the sixth, providing a glimpse of how their carpet ride arrived at this exit. After going 68 pitches between hits - Kazuo Matsui led off the game with a single - the Rockies began grinding out at-bats. Todd Helton and Atkins walked and scored on back-to-back singles by Hawpe and Yorvit Torrealba.

If nothing else, late outbursts made the eighth compelling. With Terry Francona turning into Tony La Russa - "We were hanging on for dear life," Francona said of his chess moves - Jonathan Papelbon retired Holliday on a long flyball with runners on first and second.

Holliday threw his helmet in disgust, a moment that eloquently explained the entire series.

"They have outhit us, outpitched us and outplayed us," Fogg said. "But we aren't done yet." ■

Matt Holliday watches his home run in the seventh inning make the score 6-5 Red Sox. *Andy Cross, The Denver Post*

GAME 4: At Coors Field, Denver
Red Sox 4, Rockies 3

Inning	1	2	3	4	5	6	7	8	9	runs	hits	errors
Boston	1	0	0	0	1	0	1	1	0	4	9	0
Colorado	0	0	0	0	0	0	1	2	0	3	7	0

BROOMSDAY

Colorado's miraculous late-season surge comes to a sad ending in final four games

By Troy E. Renck

October 29, 2007

Sometimes dreams, no matter how inspiring, are not enough.

The Rockies' magical season died on Sunday night, forever frozen within reach of a goal that seemed laughable when the players arrived in Tucson eight months ago. Four games, four losses. A paradise and championship lost.

The Boston Red Sox are the World Series champions after a nervy 4-3 victory Sunday night at Coors Field.

"To get this close and not win, it's hard," said first baseman Todd Helton, who waited 10 years to reach the playoffs. "When we get away from it, we will realize that we did something special."

The Rockies carried this dream for five weeks, nearly made it real. But at 10:05 p.m. the clock struck midnight and the valet brought back a pumpkin. While they became competitive — the final three games were winnable — the Rockies never got comfortable in the sport's floodlights.

They hit as if each at-bat were their last, swings more appropriate for a home run derby than the World Series. They couldn't move runners, couldn't produce quality outs, too often striking out (such was the case with runners on in the third, sixth and seventh innings).

They didn't pitch well enough, their starters only once working at least five innings, the best outing arriving too late Sunday with Aaron Cook's blue-collar performance against the Red Sox.

When needed most this weekend, their bullpen failed them. Reliever Brian Fuentes couldn't provide a shutdown inning, the gap widening to three runs in the eighth on Bobby Kielty's solo home run. Manager Clint Hurdle finally went to closer Manny Corpas to close out the inning, his loyalty to Fuentes, so rewarded in September, a painful decision Sunday when Garrett Atkins crushed a two-run home run moments later.

Colorado just never caught its breath, never gained traction. Everything was an uphill trudge, the Rockies trailing in 33 of the 36 innings.

Colorado's Legends of Fall ultimately no match for Boston's Legion of Broom.

"We weren't overwhelmed. I thought we showed we belonged," Rockies shortstop Troy Tulowitzki said. "To sit there and watch (the celebration) and know it's over is kind of shocking."

The Red Sox were too everything in winning their second title in four years. Too strong, too good, too expensive. They outscored the Rockies 29-10, outhit them 47-29.

Jon Lester worked 5 2/3 scoreless innings, Series MVP Mike Lowell homered and Jonathan Papelbon

Matt Holliday personifies the Rockies' frustration after popping out in the sixth inning. *Andy Cross, The Denver Post*

Yorvit Torrealba waits for the ball as Mike Lowell comes in for a score in the fifth inning. *Andy Cross, The Denver Post*

notched his third consecutive save.

Their pulse slow on the sport's biggest stage, their team looking every bit a $143-million bully (the Red Sox's $51.1 million posting bid for Daisuke Matsuzaka nearly equal the Rockies' $54-million payroll).

"We beat a very good team. I hope nobody forgets that," Red Sox manager Terry Francona said. "They gave us a battle to the end."

Befitting a team that forged its reputation on doing the unthinkable, the Rockies provided one final parting gift for a soldout crowd that featured loyalists and fans du jour.

With one out in the eighth, his team's only run a Brad Hawpe seventh-inning moonshot, Helton singled to left off reliever Hideki Okajima.

Up came Garrett Atkins, who has suffered through a month-long postseason cringe. He had one RBI in the playoffs, before tripling that number when he launched a 93-mph fastball into the right-field seats, shaving the deficit to 4-3.

In the ninth, Jamey Carroll nearly had Sox fans choking on their hearts in their throat, lining out at the fence on a fine play by Jacoby Ellsbury.

It only delayed the inevitable. Papelbon struck out pinch-hitter Seth Smith on a 94-mph fastball for the final out, throwing his hands and glove into the air as catcher Jason Varitek raced to the mound to bear hug him.

They stole the Rockies' scene. It was if the pixie dust evaporated during the intrasquad games and batting-cage days.

Nonetheless, these Rockies will forever be rooted in Colorado sports history, filed under goosebumps and mouths agape. They captured the imagination of a state, a region.

That will be remembered even as a sea of red fans celebrated at Coors Field deep into the night.

"When I see the pictures, I will remember what a special time this was," Helton said. "For a bunch of regular guys we accomplished a lot. I hope the city is proud of us, because I know I am." ∎

Seth Smith reacts after making the final out in the ninth inning while Jason Varitek begins Boston's celebration.

Andy Cross, The Denver Post

TRASH TALKIN'

NLCS Game 1: Rockies 5, Diamondbacks 1
Debris-tossing fans, D-backs ace can't sidetrack Colorado Francis' pitching
By Troy E. Renck

October 12, 2007

It started with a few bottles of water. Then beer containers. Before the fans at Chase Field were done Thursday night, they lost their dignity and their Arizona Diamondbacks lost control of the National League Championship Series.

During this improbable stretch, the Rockies have trumped aces, crushed closers and squashed dreams of three teams. On a warm desert night, they tiptoed through the seventh-inning litter and deposited the Diamondbacks in the trash with a 5-1 victory in Game 1.

This win brought an emotion previously absent over the past three weeks: anger. While the national media is quick to portray the Rockies as Cinderella, she never acted like this. The Rockies didn't just beat the Diamondbacks, they took off their glass slipper and pounded them between the eyes, shoving back after Justin Upton's hard seventh-inning slide spurred fans to fire debris onto the field.

"I understand why their fans got mad that (Upton was called for interference). But they don't know the rules," Rockies catcher Yorvit Torrealba said. "It was a dirty play."

The Rockies, with tempers flaring, had no problem bowing their backs. Shortstop Troy Tulowitzki exchanged words with Upton, furious that the rookie stared down starting pitcher Jeff Francis after getting hit with a pitch. Kazuo Matsui, his right knee red after the game from an ice pack, hung in on the kid's slide, refusing to give in.

It was another wrinkle to this run: talent and toughness. The Rockies won't say this game was more significant. They are too humble to hint that they just might have demoralized the Diamondbacks. But the graffiti is on the wall. The Rockies have won 18 of their past 19 games. Catch 'em if you can.

"It's crazy, it really is," said Francis, who frustrated the Diamondbacks with his ability to change speeds. "It's hard to explain."

Colorado won by slugging Arizona's Brandon Webb, the only starting pitcher who has beaten them since Sept. 15. This can't be overstated. The Diamondbacks were at home. They had swept the Chicago Cubs in their division series. This was their chance to make a statement that this was going to bare-knuckle, drawn-out brawl.

Instead, Webb weeble-wobbled and staggered through the first three innings.

"Anytime you beat Webb, it's huge," third baseman

Brad Hawpe watches the flight of his single off Arizona Diamondbacks pitcher Brandon Webb to score Kazuo Matsui and Matt Holliday during the third inning of Game 1 of the NLCS. *Eric Gay, Associated Press*

Garrett Atkins said.

By the time the sellout crowd finally arrived, the Rockies led 4-1 after three innings. Right fielder Brad Hawpe delivered the critical hit, scoring two runs with a single to right field.

The cushion, Francis admitted, helped tremendously, allowing him to pitch with more freedom. He permitted just a single run in 6 2/3 innings.

It was during an ugly seventh inning that Arizona fans brought shame to the game.

It played out like this: The Diamondbacks had runners on first and second. Augie Ojeda hit a groundball to Atkins that he flung to second baseman Matsui. Mad about getting hit by a 79 mph changeup, Upton slid late, then delivered a right forearm into Matsui's leg, upending him. First

Workers clear beer bottles off the field in the seventh inning after angry fans threw them following a close call at second base. *John Leyba, The Denver Post*

baseman Todd Helton immediately signaled that the double play be should enforced because of interference.

Second-base umpire Larry Vanover agreed. Embarrassment followed. Arizona manager Bob Melvin argued. Fans flung debris as the Rockies were ordered off the field. The eight-minute pause only delayed the inevitable. The Rockies haven't lost in a visiting park since Sept. 13, a streak spanning nine games.

The trash, in the end, amounted to a bug on the Rockies' windshield. ■

From deep left field Matt Holliday turns around and throws out Miguel Montero at second base for the third out to end the game. *RJ Sangosti, The Denver Post*

IT'S NO MIRAGE

NLCS Game 2: Rockies 3, Diamondbacks 2 {11 innings}
A bases-loaded walk to Willy Taveras in the 11th wins it, but great defense saves the day
By Troy E. Renck

October 14, 2007

Numbing is an apt description of the Rockies' 3-2, 11-inning victory in Game 2 of the National League Championship Series.

If you had asked anybody a month ago if Colorado would be two games away from the World Series, two words would have sufficed: no way.

Logic doesn't apply. There's no blueprint to this. On Friday night, the Rockies won for the 19th time in 20 games when center fielder Willy Taveras ran down a long flyball and walked to first base in the 11th on four pitches. They won when Ryan Speier recorded his first-ever major-league save. What better time than the NLCS to get his feet wet, cinching the team's 10th straight road win.

"We are playing with a lot of momentum, all 25 are in play, everybody counts or nobody counts," manager Clint Hurdle said. "We didn't draw it up that way to win our first five (playoff games), but we will take it."

As Speier struck out Arizona's Chris Young, punctuating a 4-hour, 26-minute marathon, the Diamondbacks' crowd was too tired to complain. It was a draining experience, made worse by the sobering reality confronting the D-backs. Only three teams in

postseason history have lost the first two games at home and gone on to claim the series.

"We expect to win every single game," outfielder Ryan Spilborghs said. "So to come out of here with two wins is what we expected."

Arizona doesn't seem capable of miracles, the expiration date passing in the 11th inning. Emotional in the 10th, closer Jose Valverde became volatile. Spilborghs, a pinch hitter, led off with a swinging bunt, a harmless squib that Valverde couldn't field. Slowly Valverde, the man known as Big Pappa, became the Rockies' Daddy.

He issued three consecutive walks, the most damning the last to Taveras. The Rockies' leadoff hitter reached on four straight pitches.

"I wanted to be aggressive, but he didn't throw any strikes," Taveras said.

Valverde was on foreign soil. His season-high was 32 pitches, and he finished with 42 on Friday. Arizona manager Bob Melvin defended his decision to stay with Valverde even as he ran out of gas.

"He's our closer and he was going to stay in until he gave up a run," Melvin said.

Staked to a one-run lead - recaptured after Manny Corpas blew only his second save and first since Sept.

Rockies' Willy Taveras walks to first as Ryan Spilborghs heads home during the 11th inning in Game 2 of the NLCS. *David J. Phillip, Associated Press*

21 at San Diego – Speier worked a scoreless 11th.

It was a strange ending to a game that the Rockies won with terrific defense – count 'em, six web gems by the likes of Todd Helton and Garrett Atkins – solid pitching and their ability to capitalize on mistakes (see Stephen Drew foolishly leaving the second-base bag in the ninth despite not being called out).

Rookie Ubaldo Jimenez surrendered just one run in five innings, leaving Hurdle with his toughest decision this postseason. He removed Jimenez after just 94 pitches, but he proved wise with his bullet-proof bullpen.

"It was gutsy. He pitched out of the stretch a lot, but he hung in there," Hurdle said.

Taveras, an addition to the roster for this round, was spectacular in motion or not. The seeds were planted in Tucson before he face-planted Friday in a seventh-inning diving catch.

Taveras pulled his quad so severely on Sept. 8, he didn't figure to play again, let alone contribute.

Todd Helton flips the ball to pitcher Matt Herges to get Diamondbacks Jeff Salazar at first base during the 6th inning. *Andy Cross, The Denver Post*

Taveras, who had been insisting the Rockies were a playoff team as early as April, refused to surrender to injury. So as the Rockies were putting together the greatest finishing kick since the 1965 Dodgers, Taveras went to the remote desert outpost known as the instructional league.

"He busted his butt," Rockies general manager Dan O'Dowd said. "If there were any issues along the way that reflected that, he wouldn't be here. He just put his head down and went."

Same as he did in the seventh, covering more ground than Lewis and Clark as his diving catch on a Tony Clark flyball in the gap muted a rally.

"I didn't think he crushed it. It hung up and I was able to make a great catch," Taveras said. "It's nice to be appreciated by my teammates. It's a big win for us." ∎

Ryan Speier delivers a pitch in the eleventh inning. *RJ Sangosti, Denver Post*

Chris Young shows his frustration after being called out at second during Game 2 of NLCS. *Andy Cross, The Denver Post*

NEVER A DOUBT

NLCS Game 3: Rockies 4, Diamondbacks 1
Right as rain Torrealba's three-run homer pushes amazing stretch to 20-1
By Troy E. Renck

October 15, 2007

There was never a doubt, not from the sound, not from the swing, not from the arc as it lifted through the mist and rain.

Catcher Yorvit Torrealba glanced toward the left-field stands, where his three-run home run would land, and jogged around the bases with his right arm raised. It signaled joy and triumph, the defining moment in the Rockies' 4-1 victory Sunday night over the Arizona Diamondbacks in Game 3 of the National League Championship Series.

Same as the 82-mph fastball on Torrealba's bat in the sixth inning, the Rockies are in the sweet spot, one victory tonight away from a World Series berth. Consider that a minute. With 14 games remaining in the season, they sat fourth in the wild-card race, four games back. The players knew privately they probably had to go undefeated to even sniff the playoffs.

Today, a city wakes up sharing the same grin, the same dream. The Rockies are 20-1 over the past 21 games. Not since the 1976 Cincinnati Reds has a club posted victories in its first six playoff games.

One win for the National League pennant? That seems like child's play for a team that has lost once in exactly a month.

"It's crazy if you think about it, it really is," Torrealba said as he lounged back in his chair at his locker. "That's why we don't think about it. We are just enjoying the ride."

Viewed in context with this remarkable stretch, Sunday was vintage Rockies on a night more suited for the Iditarod than baseball. They played terrific defense, turning three double plays in the first three innings, twisting the knife in Arizona's back with their cold execution.

"It seemed like every ball we hit hard, someone made a play," Arizona manager Bob Melvin said.

They continued pitching as if their rotation included Drysdale or Gibson. Josh Fogg – perfectly named for the conditions – surrendered one run in six innings. The bulletproof bullpen – Jeremy Affeldt, Brian Fuentes and Manny Corpas – was unblemished, lowering the team's postseason ERA to 1.76.

The Diamondbacks are 2-for-17 with runners in scoring position, and only one of those hits produced a run.

It's one thing for the Rockies to do this in April when no one but relatives and fantasy-league owners

Yorvit Torrealba reacts after hitting a 3-run home run in the bottom of the sixth inning. *Andy Cross, The Denver Post*

Grounds crew remove the tarp before Game 3 of the NLCS. *John Leyba, The Denver Post*

are paying attention. But this is the big stage, on which palms sweat and breathing becomes difficult. At least for some. The Rockies are bathing in this spotlight, no one more comfortable than Torrealba, who hasn't stopped smiling since he hit a home run in the wild-card tiebreaker game against the San Diego Padres on Oct. 1.

He dedicated that blast to his mom, who was at Coors Field for the game. He told her then that his next home run was for his late grandma, Aurelia Hernandez.

But contact seemed a stretch for Torrealba against Livan Hernandez in the sixth.

It was a classic, seven-pitch at-bat, Hernandez creating oohs from the crowd with 58- and 62-mph curveballs. Torrealba admitted later that he probably would have struck out had he seen that loopy

pitch again. Instead, he got a fastball that he smashed into the seats, his celebration blending passion with emotion.

"It was for my grandma," Torrealba said.

How much the shot was appreciated was obvious on the bench and from the crowd. The fans provided a curtain call, Fogg the levity.

"In the dugout afterward, I told him he was my favorite player," Fogg said. "Until (today). It could be someone else."

That's what this stretch has become – always something new, always something fresh, with the ultimate Christmas present waiting to be unwrapped as early as tonight. ◼

Diamondbacks left fielder Eric Byrnes falls back after crashing into the left field wall as Rockies' Matt Holliday's 302-foot first-inning home run is caught by fans. *Karl Gehring, The Denver Post*

WORLD CLASS!

NLCS Game 4: Rockies 6, Diamondbacks 4
Holliday's homer provides a cushion and Corpas' four-out opus saves the day as Colorado sweeps Arizona
By Troy E. Renck

October 16, 2007

It's impossible to stretch the truth. Hyperbole doesn't fit.

The Rockies, a team that was too young in April, too hurt in August and too far behind in September, are going to the World Series. Colorado flogged the Arizona Diamondbacks 6-4 on Monday night in Game 4 of the National League Championship Series, bullying into baseball's final act.

There's no need for TiVo. Or historical perspective. Let's just call this what it is: the greatest run ever for a team racing into the World Series. The Rockies are 21-1 since Sept. 15. They erased a four-game deficit in the wild-card standings. They ruined the Dodgers' season, threw Ragu on the Padres' painting and spoiled TV ratings by erasing the Phillies in the division series.

Not since the 1976 Cincinnati Reds had a team won its first seven playoff games. Big Red Machine, we present Up with Purple. Or perhaps Back in Black, the uniform of choice as the Rockies won their 10th consecutive game behind Matt Holliday's three-run home run and Manny Corpas' cold-hearted, four-out save.

The embarrassment of empty seats and the stench

of six straight losing seasons were replaced by a Polaroid 15 seasons in developing. The flashbulbs provided evidence of the moment's significance. Denver has a new sports chapter to place among the Broncos' Super Bowls and the Avalanche's Stanley Cups. The Rockies are going to the World Series, facing either the Cleveland Indians or Boston Red Sox, starting next Wednesday on the road.

"You grow up and you watch those teams on the podium and guys talk about that experience – to be part of it is unbelievable," Rockies third baseman Garrett Atkins said. "It's a dream come true and something I will never forget."

The final out – an Eric Byrnes groundout to shortstop Troy Tulowitzki – triggered an avalanche of noise and joy, the Rockies bench emptying as the crowd erupted. Tulowitzki followed his throw across the diamond and jumped into first baseman Todd Helton's arms. Holliday ran deliriously from left field, stopping and throwing his glove into the air as pitcher Josh Fogg practically tackled him.

"I'm very thankful to be a part of this," Holliday said. "To just see the fans react and be a part of this is tremendous."

For historians, the Rockies advanced to the World

Rockies players hoist the NLCS trophy during the post-game celebration. *Karl Gehring, The Denver Post*

Series at 11:38 p.m., though LoDo relied on fireworks, not watches, to singe the memory into a city's psyche.

Players piled onto the pitcher's mound, screaming, laughing, pulling on National League Champion T-shirts. The third champagne party in two weeks commenced in the dugout, spilling and draining into a clubhouse that has never been anything but empty this time of year.

What made this different is that it came with accompanying drama. It wasn't the trap door that everybody thought might appear – who loses one game in a month? – but the Rockies came within arm's destiny of reality in the eighth inning.

Colorado led 6-1, marching confidently toward its first National League pennant with footprints on the Diamondbacks' chest. Holliday, shaking free of his slump, blasted a 452-foot home run to dead center field off Micah Owings. It was the punctuation to another two-out rally – "That's where they have really excelled in this series," lamented Arizona general manager Josh Byrnes – that found pinch-hitter Seth Smith at the epicenter. Smith's two-run double cruelly landed at the feet of Arizona outfielder Eric Byrnes, who insisted that the Diamondbacks had outplayed Colorado in Phoenix.

But his jam-shot double and Holliday's moonshot home run were in danger of becoming footnotes as Manny Corpas performed the sign of the cross as he jogged out of the bullpen.

The five-run cushion had deflated to two, siphoning fear into a suddenly nervous crowd. Chris Snyder blasted a three-run home run off setup man Brian Fuentes and when Justin Upton tripled, it was left to Corpas to extend the expiration date on this miracle finish.

All he had to do was silence Tony Clark, a known Rockies killer, who has socks older than some of the Rockies' players. Corpas teetered, reaching a full count. Then, in a pitch that is symbolic of a team that has grown up before a state's eyes, the 24-year-old delivered a 77-mph slider that couldn't have broken more if it were a Frisbee.

This is Corpas at his best, impossible to unnerve.

"When we put him in as our closer in June, we thought he could do it, but we weren't sure," pitching coach Bob Apodaca said. "He has no fear of anything."

The ninth seemed simple by comparison, if you ignore the waving white towels, the Rockies' chants and a stadium that was stretched to its breaking point.

Byrnes tried a headfirst slide, but was never close, a moment capturing a series when the Rockies outscored Arizona 18-8.

"It hurts," Diamondbacks' manager Bob Melvin said.

No one in the crowd wanted to leave, and who could blame them? When the state woke up this morning, it shared the same question: Did this really happen? Did the Rockies really sweep their way into the World Series?

"I'm experiencing emotions I didn't even know I had," Helton said. "We are living the dream. Just can't explain it." ∎

Rockies fans show their enthusiasm for the Rockies. *Karl Gehring, The Denver Post*

ONE IN THE BANK

NLDS Game 1: Rockies 4, Phillies 2
Red-hot Rockies open NLDS by shutting down powerful Phillies
By Troy E. Renck

October 4, 2007

Philadelphia – It was nearing 7 p.m. as the Rockies slowly spilled out of their clubhouse and toward the team bus. If logic applied, it would have been a pumpkin.

But somewhere between walkoff home runs and chin-skidding slides, this talented team was touched by magic. There is no clock on this fairy tale, no expiration date. The Rockies, on baseball's best finishing kick in 47 years, carved up the Philadelphia Phillies 4-2 on Wednesday in the opener of the National League division series at Citizens Bank Park.

Colorado's 15th win in its last 16 games was convincing, if not a contradiction. In a ballpark filled with tasty aromas and colorful vulgarity, there was thought the Rockies would feel intimidated. Or at least a bit nervous.

Yet there was a strange dynamic at work that the coaches found noticeable as early as batting practice. After an 18-day stress test, the afternoon amounted to a day spa.

"I felt totally different, relaxed," said Todd Helton, who lined a triple on the first postseason pitch he ever saw. "The last two weeks, if we lost a game the season was over."

A defeat Wednesday would have only dug a hole, placing pressure on rookie starter Franklin Morales to deliver. But the Rockies never looked up.

Jeff Francis struck out the first four batters he faced. In the second, a flexing Colorado offense began with Helton's line drive, and nine batters and 40 Cole Hamels pitches later, the Rockies owned a 3-0 lead. Garrett Atkins lashed an RBI double, Yorvit Torrealba singled in a run and, in an at-bat that revealed the day's calm pulse, rookie Troy Tulowitzki worked a bases-loaded walk after falling behind 0-2.

"I put together my best at-bat there," Tulowitzki said. "In that situation I was happy with it."

Francis would reveal why over the next few hours. This was a Game of Shadows that had nothing to do with Barry Bonds' medicine cabinet. After the first inning, hitters from both teams admitted they had trouble picking up the ball. Not just any ball. But those with serious spin.

Torrealba, whose game-calling has earned him praise all season, picked up on the issue.

So he made a slight adjustment in his pitch selection, signaling for more curveballs. They might as

Todd Helton rounds second base after hitting a triple. *Jim McIsaac, Getty Images*

Robert Johnson, owner of Dunbar Barber Shop at 2844 Welton Street, twists away from his domino game to peek at the television. *Cyrus McCrimmon. The Denver Post*

well have been invisible.

Jimmy Rollins, Shane Victorino, Chase Utley and Ryan Howard went 0-for-11 against Francis and 0-for-15 for the game. It was the first time the top four hitters in the Philadelphia lineup had gone hitless in 273 games.

"His breaking ball was much better today, sharper than in the past," said Torrealba, who had one of the Rockies' three hits after the second inning. "He was able to do what we wanted."

The Phillies, if the local TV and radio hosts were to be believed, were going to turn the mound into Francis' grave. His craftiness wouldn't work in a game like this, not against a Philadelphia team that hit .465 in 66 at-bats this season.

"He mixed his pitches and did what he had to do," said Howard, the NL's reigning MVP.

After Francis, it got worse. The Rockies' relievers continued stepping on throats, lowering their ERA to 2.44 during this 15-1 stretch. Helton certainly wasn't worried when the bullpen door opened. His biggest concern? Figuring out what all those white specks were floating around the ballpark.

"It was lint off those towels they were waving," he said.

All the Rockies do is win, and they have become more frightening now that they are playing like they have nothing to lose.

"It was the playoffs," right fielder Brad Hawpe said, "but it was the first game we've had in a long time where we didn't feel like we were done if we didn't win." ■

Matt Holliday rounds second base after his home run in the 8th inning. *John Leyba, The Denver Post*

ALL THAT KAZ

NLDS Game 2: Rockies 10, Phillies 5
Matsui's grand slam sparks dominant win
By Troy E. Renck

October 5, 2007

Philadelphia – Adversity and anonymity rode shotgun as the Rockies sputtered in mid-September. Now, both are strangers, no longer in Colorado's cellphone circle of friends.

While the Rockies would like to forever remain the cold-nosed mutts, it is time to look beyond the sly grins, hard-to-pronounce names and clubhouse pranks and see them for what they are: the National League's best team.

By demolishing Philadelphia 10-5 on Thursday, fuel-injected by Kazuo Matsui's grand slam, the Rockies moved within one victory of advancing to their first National League Championship Series.

The Rockies have won 16 of their past 17 games, forcing a strong re-examination on merit, not the number of highlights led. Perhaps Ryan Howard summed up the past two days in Philadelphia in the ninth inning. He struck out looking on a 93 mph fastball from closer Manny Corpas. Howard stood in the batter's box for several seconds, staring in disbelief.

"It's got to stop sooner or later," Phillies Game 3 pitcher Jamie Moyer said. "They are on a roll, and

they should feel pretty good about themselves."

The Rockies have outscored their opponents 116-58 during the past 19 days. They have trailed in only 11 innings. Underdog? More like Clifford the Big Red Dog.

"Our goal is to be in the World Series," catcher Yorvit Torrealba said. "There are only two teams then. If we get in or win, they would have to talk about us, right?"

It's a weird dynamic at work among a tight knit group of players. They wouldn't mind more attention, but ultimately they are a club band that doesn't need a stadium. They have reached this point by not being concerned about how they got here.

"Winning 16 of 17 seems farfetched in some people's minds. But to us, it make sense," center fielder Ryan Spilborghs said. "Maybe we are a little crazy."

Respect arrived early Thursday. Troy Tulowitzki and Matt Holliday homered on consecutive Kyle Kendrick pitches, shoving Colorado ahead 2-0. The JumboTron showed a clip from "Miracle," with USA Olympic hockey coach Herb Brooks urging his kids to respond.

That was in the bottom of the first inning.

Kazuo Matsui connects for a grand slam in the 4th inning. *John Leyba, The Denver Post*

Thirty minutes later, the largest crowd in Citizens Bank Park history swallowed its tongue when Matsui crushed a 93 mph Kyle Lohse fastball into the right-field seats. Grand slam. Or "manrui homa" in Japanese. In any language, it was a hit that was impossible for Philadelphia to overcome.

"I have power," Matsui said with a grin.

That swing, though short and compact, amounted to a lengthy dissertation about this team. For nearly three weeks, it's always someone different wandering into the spotlight.

On Thursday, Josh Fogg went from the dragon slayer to, in his words, "the vulture," picking up the victory with two scoreless innings of relief. It was his first bullpen appearance since April 16.

Closer Manny Corpas posted his second consecutive

Josh Fogg delivers a pitch versus the Philadelphia Phillies in Game Two. Josh Fogg got the win as the Rockies defeated the Phillies 10-5. John Leyba, The Denver Post

save, the pregame H2O-on-his-jersey controversy evaporated like water off his back.

So the Rockies return to Denver, a state in a purple haze, with a clinching opportunity in a ballpark where they have won 39 of their past 54 games. Does that sound like an underdog?

"They still put us on the early game when nobody is watching, and we barely make the highlights," third baseman Garrett Atkins said. "But it doesn't matter what other people think about us. We believe in ourselves, and we know we still have work to do." ∎

Nine-year-old fan Eli Needle looks dejected after the Phillies lose. *John Leyba, The Denver Post*

LIGHTS OUT!

NLDS Game 3: Rockies 2, Phillies 1
Rockies sweep stunned Phils, roll on to NLCS vs. D-backs
By Troy E. Renck

October 7, 2007

The Rockies' faith began three weeks ago and hasn't wavered. A September push has turned the Rockies' into Legends of the Fall, Colorado trumping the Philadelphia Phillies 2-1 Saturday night to advance to the National League Championship Series.

They will face the Arizona Diamondbacks in Phoenix beginning Thursday. As the Rockies sprayed Domaine St. Michelle champagne and gulped Coors Light in the clubhouse, it felt more like a beginning than an end. It was a scene – Todd Helton drenched in celebration – that was 15 years in the making, made possible by 17 wins in their last 18 games.

"To be within one strike of being eliminated (with a San Diego win eight days ago), you start to think maybe it's our time," third baseman Garrett Atkins said. "It's things you just don't see. After a few more of those things keep happening, you start thinking maybe we are destined for this."

For a team that has toiled in obscurity – they have been on national TV more the past week than over the past two years – the final act naturally blended anonymity.

After consecutive eighth-inning singles by Atkins and Brad Hawpe, seldom-used Jeff Baker wandered into the spotlight. He had only three pinch-hit RBIs in 46 bats. He survived a frightening beanball to the face to scratch his way back onto the playoff roster.

And with the Phillies sticking with left-hander J.C. Romero rather than going to closer Brett Myers, Baker delivered. On a 1-0 count, he lashed a 90-mph fastball into right field for the decisive run.

"What do you think of that?" said Baker, known as the Bake Show to teammates.

Three outs, fireworks and a relatively tame on-field celebration later – hey, it was their second in six days – the Rockies had won their first playoff series ever.

Phillies shortstop Jimmy Rollins insisted all season that Philadelphia was the team to beat. Now the Rockies are the dream to beat.

"Baseball is all about confidence, and our confidence continues to grow with each win," outfielder Brad Hawpe said.

Saturday was not just another night on the calendar. It was circled in purple. The last time the Rockies hosted a playoff game, Bill Clinton was president and John Elway was pining for a Super Bowl ring.

Elway, as he has done for the Avalanche and Nuggets, provided the pregame boost on the Jumbo-Tron, urging a win in what has become known as Rocktober.

"It was crazy. All those fans. I love them," pitcher

The Rockies celebrate their NLDS sweep of the Phillies. *Andy Cross, The Denver Post*

Matt Herges pitches against the Phillies during Game Three. *Doug Pensinger, Getty Images*

Ubaldo Jimenez said.

Pleasantly bizarre was perhaps a more apt description. Game-time temperature was allegedly 73 degrees. It dropped to 55 within 20 minutes, a wicked wind swirling in Coors Field that turned flyballs into floating orbits for four innings.

Not long after the sellout crowd zipped its coats, the lights went out at 7:56 p.m. A 14-minute delay followed because of a computer malfunction, not a late electrical bill.

Jimenez made the Phillies, the NL's highest-scoring team, look as if they were swinging in the dark. He permitted just one hit through five innings, relying largely on his sinking fastball and big curve.

Jimenez finally gave way in the seventh, a hanging 82-mph slider to Shane Victorino that the outfielder deposited into the right-field seats the only blemish on his record.

Problem was, he had no margin for error. Jamie Moyer played the ice to Jimenez's fire. He never topped 83 mph, stepping on and off the gas with his parachute changeup. Manager Clint Hurdle watched film on Moyer before the game, stressing the importance of patience with his hitters.

The Rockies' first run came from their two best offensive players in this series – Yorvit Torrealba and Kazuo Matsui. Torrealba singled in the fifth and scored on Matsui's triple.

"It's always somebody new," Torrealba said.

It was proven as the Rockies bathed in champagne, smiling, laughing, and more than anything, wondering who's next.

"I really thought we'd win," owner Dick Monfort said. "What about these guys? They are unbelievable. I am so happy for them." ■

Jeff Baker hits a single to score Garrett Atkins in the 8th inning making the score 2-1 in Game 3 of the NLDS. *John Leyba, The Denver Post*

NLD - YES!

ROCKIES 9, PADRES 8
Rockies turn three runs in 13th inning into trip to postseason
By Troy E. Renck

October 2, 2007

The noise began building quickly, a convergence of joy and delirium. Soon the clapping started in the hallway and the Domaine Ste. Michele champagne and Coors Light sprayed his face.

At 10:28 p.m. Monday, Todd Helton entered the Rockies' clubhouse and teammate Cory Sullivan hugged him. Helton, for a second, couldn't see a thing. It was the perfect snapshot of a team that had an entire state unable to believe its eyes or slow its pulse.

The Rockies had done the unfathomable, Matt Holliday scoring on Jamey Carroll's sacrifice fly in the 13th inning, punctuating a 9-8 victory over the San Diego Padres for the National League wild card.

The Rockies are going to the postseason, opening on the road Wednesday against the Philadelphia Phillies. All they had to do was play a 163rd game for 4 hours, 40 minutes, use 10 pitchers and slay the most accomplished closer in major-league history.

"It feels better than I thought it would," Helton said in a rare quiet moment as he led his daughter Tierney toward his corner locker. "To do it with these guys, it makes it so much more meaningful."

Before the 13th inning, Helton told anyone who would listen on the bench to be patient against Padres closer Trevor Hoffman. He reminded them to let the ball travel deep, to not become the latest victim of his Bugs Bunny changeup. With the fans' throats hoarse and arms sore from waving towels, Kazuo Matsui greeted Hoffman with a double. Troy Tulowitzki followed with a shot to the left-center field gap, setting the stage for Holliday.

It was Holliday's misstep on Brian Giles' flyball in the eighth that ultimately forced extra innings. He found redemption, tripling off the right-field wall. With no outs, Helton, who had played 1,578 regular-season games without reaching the postseason, was walked. Hoffman had issues at first and third.

But his biggest problem became Carroll, a defensive substitution. After nearly quitting baseball in 2002, after losing his mother nearly two years ago, Carroll's swing popped the cork on 12 years of frustration for a city that had spent the better part of a decade watching too many losing seasons. Right fielder Giles caught the line drive and fired home.

Holliday, his chin bloodied, his right hand scratched, would say later there was no doubt he was going. The throw arrived as Holliday slid headfirst. He was kneed in the head, leaving him in a purple haze, unable to stand. Legend will say he

Jamey Carroll is congratulated after his game-winning sacrifice fly scored Matt Holliday.

Helen H. Richardson, The Denver Post

Matt Holliday looks at the dropped ball by home plate after scoring the winning run. *John Leyba, The Denver Post*

missed home plate – as text messages and TV commentators suggested.

The score and the scrum at home plate screamed something different. Fireworks went off. The Rockies ran wildly to first base to mob Carroll. Hoffman, obviously crushed, trudged off the mound, saying, "This is a burden I will have to live with."

When it comes to the Rockies, impossible is nothing. They won 14 of their final 15. Their wild-card tiebreaker was not a heartbreaker, but a heartstopper.

"Even when they were down by two runs, I honestly never lost confidence," owner Dick Monfort said. "These guys have been doing it all year. And I am telling you what, with the momentum we have, watch out."

There seems to be no limit what this team can do. The Rockies squandered 3-0 and 6-5 leads. They pounded Jake Peavy for six runs, then watched their bats turn into linguini against the Padres' bullpen.

The expiration on the miracle seemed to hit in the 13th when Jorge Julio entered and immediately erased Matt Herges' three innings of brilliance. Scott Hairston hit a two-run homer, pushing the Padres ahead 8-6.

"You may live the rest of your life and not see a better baseball game," Rockies bench coach Jamie Quirk said. "It's just unbelievable. There's no other way to explain it." ∎

Rockies pitcher Josh Fogg and catcher Yorvit Torrealba chat on the mound after Fogg gave up a grand slam home run to Padres Adrian Gonzalez in the third inning. *Helen H. Richardson, The Denver Post*

WORTHY OF AN ENCORE

ROCKIES 4, DIAMONDBACKS 3

Thanks to a Padres' defeat, the Rockies' improbable postseason run continues for at least one more game

By Troy E. Renck

October 1, 2007

Under a cloudless sky, at the end of one of the most gripping and baffling major-league seasons in recent memory, Todd Helton ran across the infield as if fleeing a swarm of bees.

He sprinted, jumped, hugged and screamed. He would say later he wasn't exactly sure what he was doing. It fit perfectly Sunday, a final electric improvisation in a month that never followed Fred Astaire dance steps.

The mild moshpit of Rockies hopping near second base after the 4-3 victory over Arizona was not a party, but rather a celebration of life.

After 13 wins in their final 14 games, after six consecutive losing seasons, the Rockies are in the play-in. It's not the playoffs, but that felt like semantics after the team completed an improbable run, erasing a four- game wild-card deficit over the final two weeks.

So the Rockies return for an encore tonight at Coors Field. They take on the San Diego Padres in prime time on TBS at 5:30 p.m. in a tiebreaker cage-match. The Rockies will start Josh Fogg opposite the Padres' Jake Peavy.

The winner advances to the postseason, traveling to Philadelphia for a Wednesday opener in the National League Division Series. The loser wonders why baseball is less sympathetic than a parking ticket.

If nothing else, the Rockies proved a single theory: If you believe in destiny, you don't believe halfway.

"We have our own opportunity. It's all up to us now," said slugger Matt Holliday. "We don't have to worry about any other people helping us out anymore."

That certainly wasn't the case Sunday when as much time was spent staring at the right-field scoreboard as the game on the field. The Rockies needed a San Diego loss to create a knot in the wild-card standings. The Padres' game started an hour earlier, and they quickly jumped out to a 3-0 lead in Milwaukee.

Brian Fuentes delivers a pitch in the 7th inning against the Arizona Diamondbacks on September 30, 2007.

John Leyba, The Denver Post

Rockies fans show support as they hang a banner between innings. *John Leyba, The Denver Post*

Slowly the Brewers chipped away, detectable by the pocket eruptions from the near-sellout crowd at Coors Field listening on radios or refreshing browsers on their cellphones. At 2:38 p.m., after a Gabe Gross triple thrust Milwaukee ahead 9-4, the crowd erupted and the Rockies' focus narrowed.

"Anytime they made noise you would naturally look up," third baseman Garrett Atkins said. "At that point, we had to finish."

It was an unusually tense game for a team that has carved out a free-spirited existence this past month. After five innings, the game was scoreless despite Arizona resting or subbing out several of its regulars. Ubaldo Jimenez was everything the Rockies hoped and more, calming nerves with his brilliance. He finished with 10 strikeouts before the bullpen took the baton in the seventh.

"The way I was throwing, I thought, 'I've got it today,'" Jimenez said.

"After that I became a fan like everyone else."

With Brian Fuentes strangling the Diamondbacks, the eighth inning became a series of wows. Garrett Atkins lined a single with the bases loaded, pushing the Rockies ahead 2-1. Brad Hawpe followed with a double to right field, shoving across the final two runs and providing a cushion that closer Manny Corpas would ultimately need.

After permitting two runs, Corpas fielded Stephen Drew's swinging bunt and threw off balance for the final out at 4 p.m. It set off Helton's memorable dance, a scene that will be burned into memories regardless of today's result.

"Hawpe said I started celebrating before he was even called out," Helton said. "I knew he was out and I just let it all out at that point. But, we aren't done yet." ∎

Todd Helton is ecstatic after getting Diamondbacks shortstop Stephen Drew out at first base to clinch the win and force a tie-breaker game against the San Diego Padres for the final wild-card playoff spot.

Helen H. Richardson, The Denver Post

THE STREAK

A 21-game salute to the Rockies

By Patrick Saunders

October 24, 2007

The Streak began when a sun-drenched crowd of just 19,161 at Coors Field pleaded for Todd Helton to make a curtain call after he hit the 300th homer of his career. At the time, it was simply a nice gesture for a longtime fan favorite at the end of a decent, but unsatisfying season.

Over the next 29 days, the Rockies won 20 more times and lost just once. They cut a swath through the National League playoffs, taking three straight from Philadelphia in the NLDS and four straight from Arizona in the NLCS. Tonight they'll play in the World Series for the first time in franchise history.

"Every night, somebody different comes through for us. It's been amazing," said Matt Holliday, MVP of the NLCS.

Somebody like Jeff Baker, whose pinch-hit RBI single in the eighth inning in Game 3 of the NLDS finished off the Phillies and moved the Rockies into the NLCS. Or somebody such as Seth Smith, who hit a key two-run bloop double down the left-field line in Game 4 of the NLCS.

Now, the team that was nine games under .500 on May 21, just four games over .500 on Sept. 15, and 4 1/2 games out of the wild-card lead with only nine games to play, is in World Series. It is a fantastic finish for the ages. The Rockies are only fifth team in the last 70 years to ride a 21-1 wave — at any point during the season. They are the first team since the 1935 Chicago Cubs to win 21 of 22 after

Sept. 1. The Rockies' 7-0 record in the 2007 playoffs matches the 1976 Reds as the only teams to do it since divisional play started in 1969. On its way to back-to-back World Series titles, the Big Red Machine finished the 1976 postseason 3-0 in the NLCS and 4-0 in the World Series. "This may never happen again," manager Clint Hurdle said. "You look at your history books, how many times has this happened so far?" What the Rockies have done will certainly take its place in Colorado sports lore, right alongside a 98-yard drive in Cleveland led by a quarterback named John Elway. "Hopefully, 50 years from now, this will be talked about the way I've heard The Drive talked about in Denver, Colorado," Hurdle said. "There will be talk of The Streak. People will ask, 'Where were you during The Streak?' "

1: SEPT. 16 AT COORS FIELD
Rockies 13, Marlins 0

"That's the first curtain call I've ever had here. It was pretty neat and special, they did it up right."

–Todd Helton, after hitting the 300th career homer

2: SEPT. 18 AT COORS FIELD
Rockies 3, Dodgers 1

"To be honest, it didn't seem like that many strikeouts, but he had everything working today."

–Catcher Yorvit Torrealba, on Jeff Francis' career-high 10 strikeouts in the first game of a doubleheader

Todd Helton connects with his 300th career home run to score three more runs in the 5th inning and put
Colorado up 11-0 shortly before a rain delay at Coors Field September 16, 2007.

Brian Brainerd, The Denver Post

3: SEPT. 18 AT COORS FIELD
Rockies 9, Dodgers 8

"It was an amazing win for us. I have never felt like that before. Ever."

—Helton, who hit a two-out, two-strike walkoff homer off Dodgers closer Takashi Saito

4: SEPT. 19 AT COORS FIELD
Rockies 6, Dodgers 5

"Everyone went a little crazy. It's getting ridiculous around here right now."

—Pitcher Josh Fogg, after Brad Hawpe's game-winning homer in the eighth inning

5: SEPT. 20 AT COORS FIELD
Rockies 9, Dodgers 4

"It's kind of funny because I've never really been in a zone like this ... The ball doesn't seem as fast right now."

—Matt Holliday, who hit his 11th homer in 12 games

6: SEPT. 21 AT PETCO PARK
Rockies 2, Padres 1 (14 innings)

"Hawpe really squared that ball up and drove it to the opposite field. You don't see lefties do that often in this park."

—Padres manager Bud Black, on Hawpe's game-winning homer

7: SEPT. 22 AT PETCO PARK
Rockies 6, Padres 2

"It does have that every game is a do-or-die feeling. It has that playoff atmosphere."

—Francis, as the Rockies' win streak reaches seven, thanks to Hawpe's 4-for-4, two-RBI day

8: SEPT. 23 AT PETCO PARK
Rockies 7, Padres 3

"We know we're playing well ... Teams know down the stretch they're going to have to bring their 'A' game to beat the Rockies."

—Shortstop Troy Tulowitzki

9: SEPT. 25 AT DODGER STADIUM
Rockies 9, Dodgers 7

"There were a lot of pieces in place, and he became the piece that pulled it all together. He's brought a fire and passion that is unique."

—Manager Clint Hurdle, on Tulowitzki, whose two-run, sixth-inning homer lifts the Rockies to their ninth straight victory

10: SEPT. 26 AT DODGER STADIUM
Rockies 2, Dodgers 0

"Oh, man. I am not taking anything away from him, but he looked easy to hit."

—L.A.'s Andy LaRoche after Fogg shuts down the Dodgers for 6 and 2/3 innings.

11: SEPT. 27 AT DODGER STADIUM
Rockies 10, Dodgers 4

"To come out on the road and not lose a game — pretty amazing. I definitely think that we have something special going on here."

—Tulowitzki, after the Rockies won their 11th straight, including six on the West Coast

12: SEPT. 29 AT COORS FIELD
Rockies 11, D-backs 1

"It was hard to watch because it was our only chance."

—Holliday, who was glued to the TV as Milwaukee's Tony Gwynn Jr. pushes the game against the Padres into extra innings with a ninth inning, two-out triple off closer Trevor Hoffman. The Brewers' victory in the 11th, coupled with the Rockies' rout, keeps the dream alive.

Young fans wait for autographs during the Rockies-Padres tie-breaker for the NL wild card at Coors Field.

H. Richardson, The Denver Post

13: SEPT. 30 AT COORS FIELD
Rockies 4, D-backs 3

"The way I was throwing, I thought, 'I've got it today.'"

—Ubaldo Jimenez, who pitched a no-hitter for six innings as the Rockies qualify for a wild-card tiebreaker thanks to another Brewers victory over San Diego

14: OCT. 1 AT COORS FIELD
Rockies 9, Padres 8 (13 innings)

"I don't know if he's all right. I just saw him lying on the ground. But this whole thing is unreal. I can't believe it."

—Leslee Holliday, after watching her husband Matt crash land at home plate with the winning run, moving the Rockies into the playoffs

NL DIVISION SERIES
15: OCT. 3 AT CITIZENS BANK PARK
Rockies 4, Phillies 2

"It is what it is. (Francis) obviously did a great job. I'm not going to take anything away from him, and I'm not going to make any excuses."

—Phillies shortstop and MVP candidate Jimmy Rollins, after the top four batters in their lineup combined to go 0-for-15 with nine strikeouts

16: OCT. 4 AT CITIZENS BANK PARK
Rockies 10, Phillies 5

"After I hit it, I knew it was gone."

—Kazuo Matsui, on his grand slam. Matsui falls a single short of the cycle, joining Willie Mays as the only players with a double, triple and home run in a post-season game.

17: OCT. 6 AT COORS FIELD
Rockies 2, Phillies 1

"I just knew that I was a versatile player who could help out. All season, I just came to the park ready to play, whenever they called on me."

—Pinch-hitter Jeff Baker, whose RBI single in the eighth inning gave the Rockies a series sweep and their first trip to the National League Championship Series in franchise history

NL CHAMPIONSHIP SERIES
18: OCT. 11 AT CHASE FIELD
Rockies 5, D-backs 1

"Plastic bottles don't hurt too bad. You know, if they start throwing baseballs at me, I'd be a little nervous."

—Holliday, responding to Arizona fans who littered the field with debris after the D-backs' Justin Upton was called out for interference at second base

19: OCT. 12 AT CHASE FIELD
Rockies 3, D-backs 2 (11 innings)

"I didn't think he crushed it. It hung up and I was able to make a great catch."

—Center fielder Willy Taveras, who made a diving catch in the seventh inning on Tony Clark's flyball into the gap. In the 11th, Taveras drew a bases-loaded walk off closer Jose Valverde to drive in the winning run.

20: OCT. 14 AT COORS FIELD
Rockies 4, D-backs 1

"Those guys are really hot right now. You throw them eggs, they're going to be fried."

—D-backs starter Livan Hernandez, who gave up a decisive three-run homer in the sixth inning to Torrealba

21: OCT. 15 AT COORS FIELD
Rockies 6, D-backs 4

"I'm experiencing emotions I didn't even know I had. We are living a dream. Just can't explain it."

—Helton, who seems stunned that he's in the World Series after more than 10 seasons in the big leagues.

Hope is alive for the Colorado Rockies baseball team on October 1, 2007, as tickets sell out at Coors Field for tonight's tie-breaking game against the Padres. *Kathryn Scott Osler, The Denver Post*

REMARKABLE ROCKIES' MAGIC NUMBER IS 64

By Mark Kiszla • Denver Post Staff Columnist

October 14, 2007

At the top of the Rockies' lineup card, manager Clint Hurdle discreetly scrawls a tiny "64," circles the magic number and carries it near his heart night after miraculous night, as his team plays winning baseball that defies history and logic.

How to explain why the mysterious 64 means everything to a team doing what Babe Ruth or Sandy Koufax never dreamed?

It's a tale of wonder that must begin with a brave, dead boy.

"His name is Kyle," said Hurdle, elbows propped on the dugout railing, his face so heavy with emotion it pushes the manager's stare to the floor. "He's a hero to me."

Kyle Blakeman was a 15-year-old sophomore from ThunderRidge High School, a suburban kid who loved baseball and mac 'n' cheese. Late in summer, when the Rockies had swung big yet appeared on the verge of missing the playoffs for a 12th straight sea-

son, Blakeman died from a puzzling, rare cancer at 7:45 on the final Tuesday evening of August.

While packing for heaven, Blakeman left the Rockies a gift by handing devil-may-care underdogs roaring fearlessly toward the World Series the power of 64.

"This is a story of a kid you want the world to hear," said Joanna Blakeman, whose late son proves it's possible to find a hero on any street in America.

How has a Colorado team the baseball nation could not locate on a map, managed by a skipper with such a long history of failure his contract extension on opening day elicited catcalls, suddenly morphed into a combo of the 1927 Yankees' invincibility and jump-out-of-the-seat improbability of the '51 Giants?

All it requires is suspension of disbelief. Faith can touch you anywhere, even the grocery store, where a tap on the shoulder by a stranger introduced Hurdle to a sick teenager two years ago. Genuine friendship blossomed.

Macie Blakeman, 10, holds a photograph of her brother, Kyle, with her father, Brad, and mother, Joanna. The Blakemans lost Kyle, 15, to a rare form of cancer in August. Kyle, a hero to the Rockies' Clint Hurdle, wore No. 64 in football. Nathan W. Armes, *Special to The Denver Post*

The Blakeman family – Brad, Joanna and 10-year-old Macie – looks at photographs of Macie's older brother Kyle and Rockies manager Clint Hurdle.

Nathan W. Armes, The Denver Post

Which is why Hurdle and Blakeman found themselves staring at each other across a hospital bed on Aug. 24, knowing it could be the last of at least 20 conversations between two baseball lovers.

"Give me something here to take the team some luck. You got a little?" Hurdle recalled asking Blakeman, after a loss to Pittsburgh had incited an ugly press conference with badgering questions about the debilitating loss.

"Luck? Oh, yeah," Blakeman told the manager. The kid possessed quiet courage and unbreakable toughness to the nth degree. A hospice bed, however, seemed a weird place for a slumping 66-64 ballclub with fading postseason dreams to search for good fortune.

"He looked at me like I was full of it," Hurdle recalled.

Blakeman, ever game, played along when the man-ager asked: "Got a favorite number?"

The kid said he had always worn No. 64 on the football field.

Perfect.

So Hurdle scribbled "64" on the top of the lineup card he filled out for the very next game at Coors Field, against Washington.

And no Hollywood screenwriter could dream what happened. In the bottom of the ninth inning, with the Rockies trailing by four runs, slugger Matt Holliday smacked a home run to spark a rally. Colorado won 6-5.

Clint Hurdle's lineup card has the number "64" circled. It is a tribute to Kyle Blakeman, who died of cancer at the age of 15. *John Leyba, The Denver Post*

"I walked back in the hospital that night with this look on my face, and the nurses and family members are laughing at me, saying: 'What? You didn't think it would work?'" said Hurdle, who arrived past 11 p.m. to deliver the lineup card to his young buddy.

Within five days, the boy succumbed to renal medullary carcinoma, which attacks the kidneys first. Never heard of the disease? Only 100 cases have been confirmed worldwide. Doctors don't understand much about this cancer, except it strikes victims born with the sickle cell trait and usually kills within weeks.

"We hid what kind of cancer he had from everyone; we didn't even tell Kyle," said Joanna Blakeman, calling the day in 2005 she heard the diagnosis the worst moment of her life. "Because when you look it up in the medical books, it says: terminal. As parents, we didn't want him to live with that fear. We wanted

Macie Blakeman throws out ceremonial first pitch of Game Four of the National League Championship Series between the Rockies and Diamondbacks.
John Leyba, The Denver Post

him to be a teenager."

While a grieving mother's tears still wash over her in waves, Joanna knows her son ran off a miracle streak, making the Kid Rocks winning 19 of 20 games seem like child's play.

Last spring, with cancer in remission after aggressive treatment that included a double stem cell transplant, Kyle was back in school. Made the freshman baseball team as a third baseman. Which was the second best news he received that day. Hurdle had been on the phone at 6 a.m. wanting to yak sports.

"You and me are members of the same club, buddy.

Kyle Blakeman, who attended ThunderRidge High School, played football but also loved baseball.

Photo courtesy of the Blakeman family

I beat the disease. And so did you," ThunderRidge coach Gary Bishop, a prostate cancer survivor, would tell his young infielder. "Then," Blakeman countered, in the baseball tradition of friendly needling, "you must be the president of the club. Because you're a lot older than me."

What's the shelf life of a miracle? Carpe diem gets only so many swings of the bat.

The cancer returned with a vengeance during the summer.

In six weeks, Kyle was gone.

At the funeral, Bishop caught the eye of mourning parents and thought: "Boy, this old dog got lucky. I got the chance to coach your son."

See? The magic of 64 really is luck. The luck you make goes beyond a diving catch by Rockies outfielder Willy Taveras or walking home with the winning run in the 11th inning.

Baseball ain't nothing but a game, and is playoff tension anything to fear? When a mom calls and asks you to stop by the hospital "to see her son before he

Manager Clint Hurdle looks on from the dugout prior to the Rockies game against the Phillies.

Cyrus McCrimmon, The Denver Post

was going to pass that night," Hurdle said. "That was debilitating."

Before Game 3 of the National League Championship Series against Arizona, Hurdle will double-check the details of his starting lineup, and circle the only number that really matters.

"I'm embarrassed to admit this," said a blushing mother, chuckling. "But that special lineup card Clint brought Kyle in the hospital? It's so special we put it away somewhere in the house, and now we can't find it."

No worries.

The Rockies will make more tributes to Kyle Blakeman, by seizing the little miracles that can be found anytime, anywhere.

"We're going to keep on writing 64 on the lineup card," Hurdle said. "Why stop now?" ■

Kyle Blakeman pictured in his baseball uniform. *Photo courtesy of the Blakeman family*

ROCKIES FOCUS

Rockies' success rides on Holliday leading a wave of young talent

By Patrick Saunders

April 1, 2007

Matt Holliday was sprawled on the lawn outside the Rockies' spring training clubhouse at Hi Corbett Field.

His wife, Leslee, sat beside him, cradling their newborn son, Ethan. Holliday grinned as he watched his 4-year-old son, Jackson, play a ragtag baseball game with a bunch of kids. It was an idyllic scene, far removed from the Rockies' second-half meltdown of last summer. And the peaceful moment gave no hint of what's at stake for Holliday and his team this season.

For years, the Rockies have begged fans for patience with promises of young talent on the way from the farm. Now it's high noon at 20th and Blake.

Throughout Denver's cold, harsh winter, the club preached a win-now mentality. From owner Charlie Monfort to manager Clint Hurdle to the longtime face of the franchise, Todd Helton, the mantra has been, "Shut up and play."

Jobs, specifically general manger Dan O'Dowd's and Hurdle's, are likely tied to success or failure in 2007. The plan to win has come into focus, those in the organization firmly believe.

If Holliday feels the weight of expectations on his broad shoulders, he doesn't show it.

"I feel great about everything," he said. "I feel good

personally, and I feel good about where we're going as a team. This is my fourth season here, and it's by far our best team. How that translates to wins is yet to be found out."

The Rockies were 44-43 at the all-star break last season. They appeared to be contenders in a lackluster National League West. But they quickly reverted to pretender status, going 32-43 (.427) after the break, the worst record in the National League.

Led by their Generation R poster boys – pitchers Aaron Cook and Jeff Francis, third baseman Garrett Atkins, right fielder Brad Hawpe and Holliday – the Rockies were not ready for prime time.

Now, even with the addition of two rookies in the starting lineup, Troy Tulowitzki at shortstop and Chris Iannetta at catcher, the Rockies quietly say they're ready to turn the corner.

"We have to do what we did from the beginning of the season until July 5 last year," Hurdle said. "That means relying upon one another. We'll play smart and play hard, and play with passion."

Skepticism is easy when it comes to the Rockies, who haven't had a winning season since 2000. Home attendance has dropped from among the best to 23rd in the majors a year ago, when Colorado averaged

Brad Hawpe is in the batting cage for practice during spring training at Hi Corbett Field in Tucson.

Hyoung Chang, The Denver Post

Opening Day at Coors Field where the Rockies met the Diamondbacks. *Cyrus McCrimmon, The Denver Post*

25,980 fans, second-lowest in franchise history.

Ownership has indicated payroll will be increased only if attendance and revenue go up. That likely will be the only way the Rockies hold on to – for a few seasons at least – budding stars such as Holliday and Atkins. Holliday, 27, is the first and brightest star to emerge from the Rockies' recent homegrown strategy. It's fitting that his future in Colorado rides on the Rockies' ability to attract more fans and generate more revenue. He made $500,000 last year. A new, one-year contract pays him $4.4 million this season. He isn't eligible for free agency until after the 2009 season, and until then the team can go year-to-year in salary arbitration, as it did this season.

With Holliday's salary expected to soar in future years, the Rockies' ability to afford him is tied to on-field success – and bringing the fans back.

"If we go out and compete into September and possibly compete for the playoffs, that will definitely show that we are taking huge steps in the right direction," Holliday said. "The attendance will be up, and revenue will increase. But what the owners do with that is their decision. All I can do is be the best player I can be."

Last season, Holliday became an all-star for the first time, hitting .326 with 34 homers and 114 RBIs. Hurdle says he will be satisfied if Holliday matches those numbers. Helton is convinced Holliday will do better.

"When a guy comes off a season like that, the one thing you worry about is if he stops working, gets rusty and sits on the season he had," Helton said. "There's just no way that will happen. It's just not in Matt's vocabulary. He's a hard-working guy who takes care of his body and has a lot of pride. He'll be ready."

Added Hurdle: "All-star status is not a burden for Matt. It's something that he carries well, and he's a ballplayer who wants to go out and get better."

Although Holliday smashes tape-measure homers and is well-respected by teammates, he's not a vocal leader or a clubhouse cutup. Nor is he eager to sup-

Rockies Manager Clint Hurdle watches batting practice before the preseason game against Chicago White Sox at Hi Corbett Field. *Hyoung Chang, The Denver Post*

plant Helton as the face of the franchise.

"I wouldn't say that this is Matt Holliday's team, but I like the fact that Garrett and myself and some of the guys can take some of the burden off Todd," Holliday said. "I like that. I hope he feels like he doesn't have to carry us. He can have an off day and we can still win. From that aspect, I'm happy that me and Garrett and Hawpe can take some of the burden off his shoulders."

Holliday, as good as he is, realizes he has room for improvement. Like his teammates, he often struggled in the clutch. He hit .200 with runners in scoring position and two outs.

And, while he ranked seventh among National League left fielders with a .979 fielding percentage, his outfield play was at times a nail-biting adventure.

"I feel like I can get better in all areas," Holliday said. "I've really worked hard on my defense this spring. I want to be a more complete player."

Hurdle sees a young player coming into his prime, much as he hopes his young team does.

Jeff Francis, left, and Aaron Cook, make Brad Hawpe smile during the photo day at Hi Corbett Field.

Hyoung Chang, The Denver Post

"I've seen him take steps forward in a lot of different areas," Hurdle said. "Baserunning is something he wants to improve on. And he's emerged in the clubhouse, too. He's a quiet leader, not a pompom-waving kind of guy. But he also likes to have fun. He has a youthful zest to him that's refreshing."

For the first time, Holliday and his family stayed in Denver during the offseason. It's home. For how long, he doesn't know. It might depend on how well the Rockies do in realizing their vision.

"All I'm thinking about is this season and this team," he said. "These guys are some of the best friends I will ever have. We are very close. I don't know how that translates to wins, but we know each other and rely on each other. I think we've got a chance to be good. I really do." ∎

Troy Tulowitzki does some infield work during the Colorado Rockies Spring Training. *Hyoung Chang, The Denver Post*

BROOMTOWN

ROCKIES 4, YANKEES 3
Atkins, Tulowitzki homer to make it bummer of trip for vaunted Bronx Bombers
By Troy E. Renck

June 22, 2007

At 9:30 a.m. Thursday, a battery of friends sat outside Coors Field with cheap beer, warm smiles and brooms. And they weren't the cleaning crew.

They were waiting for Rockpile tickets. To cheer the home team. Imagine that.

The Rockies rewarded their faith with a comic book finish. The Legends of Fall were no match for the Legion of Broom.

The Rockies swept the New York Yankees with a 4-3 victory before a third consecutive sellout crowd, sweeping a series that nobody thought they were going to win, let alone dominate.

With a baby-faced shortstop, a gritty starting pitcher and less winning tradition than a leftover sock at Yankee Stadium, the Rockies spotted New York two runs, then knocked out Roger Clemens. Just a month ago, there was talk of Colorado sinking in quicksand.

At 18-27, the Rockies were one of the National League's worst teams.

Thursday, they rode off in buses for a 10-day road trip just 3 1/2 games behind the division-leading San Diego Padres, all but cackling at ruining the Yankees'

hyped visit to Denver.

"To sweep any team is a great," said Rodrigo Lopez, who remained undefeated, surrendering two runs in 5 2/3 innings. "But to sweep the Yankees with all that mystique, we made a statement."

Not that the Yankees' arrival was a big deal, but you had to check to make sure that John, Paul, George and Ringo weren't in the starting lineup.

Had the Rockies just won three straight over the Yankees, it would have been surprising. But they spent three days muffling them in bubble wrap, part of a stretch that has seen them go a baseball-best 20-7.

The previous time the Yankees were here, in 2002, they scored 41 runs. This week, they managed five.

"I would have lost a lot on that (bet)," Clemens said.

In their previous visit, they totaled 54 hits. This time? One hit with runners in scoring position.

"A lot of people who came here Tuesday to cheer them left unhappy (Thursday)," third baseman Garrett Atkins said. "That's a good feeling."

The Yankees' 2-0 lead evaporated on home runs by shortstop Troy Tulowitzki and Atkins. A laboring Clemens exited after recording just 13 outs, failing to record his 350th victory. The loss was secured to his

With broom in hand, Curtis Trujillo, 21, celebrates the Rockies' sweep over the Yankees after the third and last game of the three game Rockies-Yankees series. *Brian Brainerd, The Denver Post*

name in the sixth when Rockies reliever Jorge Julio fanned Hideki Matsui on a nasty slider with runners on first and second.

"I think this team has a good chance to go to the playoffs. You know why?" Julio asked. "Because we have a great bullpen (4.25 ERA). Our starters go six, seven innings, nobody has a chance."

The challenge for the Rockies is to contend for six months, prove they are a good team, not just a club that got alarmingly hot.

They face Toronto – a favorable matchup since they

Kazuo Matsui tags out Derek Jeter between second and third base after Alex Rodriguez reaches first on a fielder's choice. *John Leyba, The Denver Post*

are 9-3 against the AL East this season – the Chicago Cubs and Houston Astros. Given the way the Rockies have played on the road since May 21 (9-2), they might find a line of Rockpile fans when they return.

"We have to prove it over time," Matt Holliday said. "It's just hot air if we don't play well the rest of the year." ■

Troy Tulowitzki watches his home run to left center on a 3-2 pitch in the second inning. *John Leyba, The Denver Post*

NEXT NATIONAL HOLLIDAY

Value of young Rockies outfielder growing with all-star talent
By Troy E. Renck

July 8, 2007

The question no longer seems to be whether the Rockies can afford Matt Holliday, but whether they can afford to lose him.

In his fourth full season in the big leagues, Holliday has evolved from a pedestrian prospect into a reincarnation of Dante Bichette, with a much better glove. The left fielder led the National League in hitting .340, RBIs and finished with 36 home runs, good enough to put him in a strong contention to win the NL MVP honors.

At 27, the kid is a man now, unstoppable as a Colorado winter and a larger-than-life figure at Coors Field.

"The first exposure to him is that every time you look on the scoreboard, he's among the league leaders in all categories," Yankees manager Joe Torre said. "Then you see him on TV. But you don't realize how big is he until he steps into that batter's box. Or, frankly, how good he is."

And yet Holliday lives in relative anonymity. Not that he was overlooked or anything, but fans needed OnStar to find his name on the all-star ballot this past season. He made his second consecutive appearance in the Midsummer Classic because his peers noticed. No National Leaguer received more votes from players than Holliday, who put on a show in the Home Run Derby.

"The biggest thing that hurts him is that he plays in Colorado. I don't think the rest of the country has any idea how good he really is," Mets pitcher Tom Glavine said at midseason. "I think you are going to see the word spread more and more. Pretty soon he's going to be a guy that teams aren't going to let beat them."

Not since Todd Helton has a young Rockies player gotten this good, this fast. It has created a strange dynamic, with fans worried Holliday will be saying goodbye just as they are learning to say hello. Nineteen months ago, Holliday switched agents, hiring Scott Boras, effectively, and Holliday believes unfairly, altering the perception of him.

"I have to sign with somebody if I want to keep playing baseball, right? I don't think that has anything to do with me staying here or not," Holliday said. "I hired him because I think he's the best at what he does. I didn't hire him to get me out of

Matt Holliday waves to the crowd after he hit a three-run homer in the fourth inning of Game 4 of the NLCS.

Andy Cross, The Denver Post

Matt Holliday watches his home run in the first inning in Game 2. *John Leyba, The Denver Post*

Denver or get me the biggest contract in baseball history. I hired him because he has my best interests at heart, and he's a genius at what he does. There will be a lot of factors involved."

Entering this season, critics suggested Holliday was replaceable. He was viewed as a defensive liability and a Coors Field Frankenstein. Holliday spent the season debunking that argument. His routes have improved dramatically on flyballs, hardly an accident after dropping to 230 pounds and working extensively on his positioning during the season with Rockies outfield coach Glenallen Hill.

"He's put the time in," Hill said. "Give him the credit."

Offensively, Holliday emerged as a Triple Crown threat.

"I feel like I am doing a better job of calming my nerves and handling situations better," Holliday said during the season.

No one is less surprised by Holliday's transformation than his brother Josh, the hitting instructor at Arizona State. Josh said when Matt was 15, the family realized he was going to be a pro athlete. Back then the family figured it might be in the NFL since Holliday left high school in Stillwater, Okla., as the nation's second-highest recruited quarterback behind Ronald Curry and ahead of Carson Palmer.

"He has so much pride in what he does. He will work at something until he gets it right," Josh said. "We are

Herbie Schwein, 13, of Highlands Ranch cheers Holliday's 1st inning home run in Game Three of the NLCS.

Glenn Asakawa, The Denver Post

Matt Holliday with his three-year-old son Jackson after the game. *John Leyba, The Denver Post*

so proud of him. And he hasn't changed a bit. He's a great brother, husband and father. He's still Matt to us."

His teammates call him "Big Daddy" because of his Popeye-sized forearms and enormous physique. But there's a charming innocence to Holliday that gets lost in his super-sized stats. Few know that he grew up with pictures of Cal Ripken Jr. on his bedroom wall. His dog, in fact, was named Cally after the Baltimore Orioles' Hall of Famer.

He loves and lives baseball, never more comfortable than on the Fourth of July. While a sellout crowd at Coors Field was enjoying fireworks, Holliday was pitching to his son Jackson in the Rockies' indoor batting cage. Afterward, he walked to a nearby restaurant through a couple thousand people and nobody recognized him.

"And it didn't bother me one bit," Holliday said.

The simplicity, the sunflower seeds in the mouth, the toothy smile are all part of his appeal. It's becoming hard to put a price tag on the MVP of the National League Championship Series.

"Todd (Helton) is the face of the franchise and as long as he's here, he should be. He deserves it and I don't necessarily want it," Holliday said. " I just want to play baseball." ∎

Matt Holliday gets hit by a pitch in the third inning. Game four of the NLCS. *Andy Cross, The Denver Post*

WIN WITH TULO-WHIZ KID

Losing never an acceptable option for Rockies' star rookie shortstop

By Troy E. Renck

October 23, 2007

Take a look. The lime-green T-shirt peeks outside of his black sweat shirt. Don't stare. Just a subtle glance is necessary.

The word "Boston" emblazons the front in cheesy white letters. This faded, well-worn garb is the last reminder that Troy Tulowitzki is a rookie.

It was reluctantly purchased as part of a June field trip along the Freedom Trail in Boston.

"It was boring," Tulowitzki, 23, said with a smile Monday.

A fashion hazing incident is the only way to know Tulowitzki is a kid. As the Rockies prepare to open the World Series on Wednesday night at Fenway Park, Tulo is attempting to become the first rookie shortstop to win a ring since the New York Yankees' Derek Jeter in 1996. Tulowitzki wears No. 2 because of Jeter. The similarities go beyond the number on their backs.

Tulowitzki, more than anything else, is a winner, that rare athlete capable of making those around him better.

"He's not the leader of the clubhouse yet, because we won't let him. Eventually, he will be," pitcher Josh Fogg said. "He has that kind of personality where people gravitate toward him. He still has the enthusiasm of a Little Leaguer. A really good Little Leaguer who wants to win every game."

Titles define careers. October performances frame a reputation nationally. Tulowitzki realized this long ago when he began watching Cal Ripken – the reason he played shortstop – then later Nomar Garciaparra and Jeter. People love great players, but they remember champions.

"That's why you play, right?" Tulowitzki said.

All Tulowitzki did in his first season is put together the greatest season ever by a NL rookie shortstop, hitting .291 with 24 home runs and 99 RBIs. He committed just 11 errors and led the league in putouts.

Even more impressive, when the Rockies sat at 18-27 entering May 22, Tulowitzki spoke up.

"This is disturbing," he said. "I could never get used to this."

To understand how Tulowitzki got here, it helps to understand his upbringing in Sunnyvale, Calif., a suburb of San Jose. Father Ken's early recollections

Tulowitzki celebrates with teammates after knocking in the game-winning run against the Houston Astros.

Karl Gehring, The Denver Post

Troy Tulowitzki gets a high five from first baseman Todd Helton, left, after tying the score 8-8 in the 13th inning. *Helen H. Richardson, The Denver Post*

provide a glimpse of young Tulo. After work, Dad and friends would play cards or board games.

"If Troy lost, he would get upset and insist that the guys cheated," Ken said from his home.

Sports were a natural outlet for Troy, a perfect fit where he could more easily control the outcome. Troy began his baseball career with the Sunnyvale Orioles as a 7-year-old. He always played shortstop and pitched. He had an arm even then that made folks pay attention.

By 8, it was becoming difficult to ignore Troy's talent. He was on the Padres that season, Dad remembers. And Troy had a problem.

He was, to put it politely, a ball hog, which is much more difficult in baseball than basketball. As far as he was concerned, anything hit to second or third was his as well as what was directed to shortstop.

"I would ask him why he kept doing it and he said, 'Because those other guys can't catch,'" Ken recalled. "He wasn't being mean. He just wanted to get all the

outs. The parents would get a little upset, and I remember someone telling him to stop throwing so hard to first base. Troy said, 'Why don't you put someone over that can catch?'"

According to Ken, the league agreed. They held an emergency meeting, voting to allowing Troy to play up rather than allow him to remain a health hazard for kids with toy gloves.

"My dad never told me any of that while it was going on," Troy said. "I just wanted to play."

Winning became a habit, not a coincidence.

Troy has never been on a team with a losing record. He played in Pop Warner national football tournaments, became a scoring threat in hoops through high school and, along with Padres farmhand Robert Perry, helped Sunnyvale place second in the Little

Troy Tulowitzki

Troy Tulowitzki turns a double play in the second inning of Game 3 of the NLCS. *Andy Cross, The Denver Post*

A Magical Season

In the fifth inning Troy Tulowitzki ran down this Brandon Webb hit to get out the Arizona pitcher.

Cyrus McCrimmon, The Denver Post

League West Region tournament in 1997 and third in the Senior Little League World Series in 2001.

"He's old-school, and you don't hear that term very much anymore," said Rockies Triple-A hitting instructor Carney Lansford, whose son Josh played with Tulowitzki on all-star teams. "He's the same now as when I saw him years ago. He could have played in any era."

While Tulowitzki was always a star, he was motivated by failure. He wasn't drafted out of high school, considered too skinny at 180 pounds. He was recruited, landing at Long Beach State, but not considered a prize. Thinking back brings a sly grin.

"I know of a couple of (big-league) area scouts that told me they got fired for not telling their teams to take a chance on me," Tulowitzki said. "I am not happy they lost their jobs, but ..."

Don't tell him can't do something.

He's burning to show he can hit in the playoffs, his .179 average with 10 strikeouts "terrible," in his own word. That inner drive surfaced when he was drafted in the first round by the Rockies in 2005.

Upon arriving in Denver with his father, a Rockies employee showed the kid around to the local eateries and attractions, finishing with a trip to the field.

Colorado lost that day, and the team official said, according to Ken, that's just the way it is around here.

"Troy didn't like that," Ken said. "I remember friends telling me that it was too bad the Rockies drafted him. I said, 'We'll see what happens when he gets to the big leagues.'"

Since claiming the starting job in spring training – it was unofficially his when he got into pitcher Denny Bautista's face on March 4 as a game began to

spin out of control – he has earned the respect of teammates, opponents and legends. Todd Helton calls him the "team catalyst." Manager Clint Hurdle said he's "the extra-special sauce that brought the flavor out in everything."

Garciaparra raved about how seriously Tulowitzki took his craft, while Ripken gushed at the kid's positioning.

"He's a true student of the game," Ripken said.

That Ripken took time out to talk to Troy last week amazed his dad. It seems like just yesterday that he was taking his boy to the Oakland Coliseum to watch Ripken play. He can't wait to hear the story. But there's another chapter still to write.

"I haven't bothered him during this run," Ken said, "because I know he's focused on one thing: winning." ■

Rockies celebrate after beating the Phillies during the third game of the division series. *RJ Sangosti, The Denver Post*

HELTON TOWERS

First baseman remains the acknowledged face of the franchise despite
a reduction in his once-formidable power stats

By Patrick Saunders, The Denver Post

July 9, 2007

The Rockies' resident perfectionist has made self-evaluation an art form.

But Todd Helton doesn't like to talk about himself.

Ask him about the state of the Rockies at the all-star break and he opens up a bit, saying he believes they will be legitimate contenders in the National League West come August and September.

"We're resilient," he said. "We've had plenty of opportunities to be sitting 15 games below .500 right now, but we're not. That tells you something."

Ask Helton about the strides made by Brad Hawpe, and he gushes with praise: "He's been crazy good. He's made amazing strides. He's one of those hitters, and there are very few of them, that when he's at the plate, you expect something really good is going to happen."

But ask him to analyze his own first half of the season and Helton provides cloudy answers.

"There are pluses and minuses," he said. "I'm well aware of what I'm doing well, and I'm well aware of what I need to do better."

Dare ask the 33-year-old about his declining power and he bristles.

"What do you want me to say?" he said. "I'm just going out there trying my best every day, whether I hit a home run or strike out. You think I work my butt off all season for seven home runs?"

Make that eight. Helton hit a solo shot Sunday in the Rockies' 8-4 loss to the Phillies. He heads into the break with a .313 average, 49 RBIs and 20 doubles. His .444 on-base percentage ranks second in the NL. Those are good numbers for most players, but below par for someone who entered the season hitting .333 for his career and who has averaged 46 doubles and 25 homers a season.

Helton, bulked up and healthy after illness crippled much of his 2006 season, rushed out of the gate, hitting .384 in April. On May 11, he was hitting .397. Since then, he has hit .257.

Manager Clint Hurdle, always one of Helton's biggest supporters, believes fixes are in the works, and cites Helton's double off the right-field wall Saturday night and his homer Sunday as progress.

"I think Todd has plenty left," Hurdle said. "I think there is power there that he hasn't been able to unleash, just because of mechanics. Is there a decline in power? Yes. But is it correctable? Yes. Is there still power? Yes. I think he'll get it right."

Philadelphia manager Charlie Manuel, who watched Helton go 5-for-12 in three games against the Phillies, still considers him dangerous. "I know

Todd Helton pumped his fist in the air after watching his ninth-inning homer clear the fence to win the game Tuesday night. *Karl Gehring, The Denver Post*

that he's a guy who's going to make solid contact, he's going to get on base and he's always a threat," Manuel said Sunday. "He doesn't hit homers the way he used to, but we sure take notice of him."

That said, Manuel has observed changes over the years.

"I think as he's gotten older, he's become more of a line-drive hitter," Manuel said. "I think when he was younger, he got more balls up in the air. He doesn't get the slight little lift like he used to. But when it's all said and done, I think he's capable of 25 to 30 home runs, if he stays healthy."

Two-time all-star outfielder Matt Holliday is the Rockies' emerging star, but he happily acknowledges that Helton remains the face of the franchise. Holliday says Helton's value can't be measured in raw statistics.

Todd Helton looks on with a smile before the start of their game with the Phillies in the NLDS.

John Leyba, The Denver Post

"His presence is invaluable, and he's still one of the best fielders in the game," Holliday said. "He's been around a long time and thrived for a long time, so he knows what it takes to be great. I think that commands respect in our clubhouse. Plus, I think his presence in the lineup is still huge and affects how all of us get pitched."

Helton, tougher on himself than anyone else could possibly be, claims he doesn't let critics get to him.

"It's like a fan yelling something at me at an opposing ballpark," he said. "I mean, they are welcome to have their opinion, but I don't let it affect me. I'll just keep working at my job. That's all I can do." ∎

Rockies fans hold up signs as Colorado Rockies Todd Helton comes out of the dugout for batting practice.

John Leyba, The Denver Post

FRANCIS WORKS WAY TO TOP

By Patrick Saunders, The Denver Post

August 26, 2007

It was late in the Rockies' dispiriting 5-1 loss to Pittsburgh on Thursday afternoon when a kernel of optimism popped in Jamey Carroll's head.

"Just knowing Jeff was going to pitch tomorrow, I immediately thought, 'We'll get a lot of strong innings,'" the Rockies' utilityman said. "I knew we had an opportunity to win."

The Rockies did win the next day, though Francis did not get a decison. It was Francis, however, who anchored a starting staff ravaged by injuries and led them to the postseason when hope appeared lost.

"If you're an elite pitcher, you have to be good every time out," said Francis, who tied a club record with 17 victories and won Game 1 of the NLDS and the NLCS sweeps. "But I like the challenge of that, because I do expect to go out and do things to help this team win every time I pitch."

The 6-foot-5 lefty has become the Boy Scout of Rockies starting pitchers: solid, reliable and always prepared. On the mound, the 26-year-old Canadian appears unflappable and analytical. But those characteristics camouflage his raw competitiveness and

desire to step up in class and join aces such as San Diego's Jake Peavy, Arizona's Brandon Webb and Minnesota's Johan Santana.

Francis finished 17-9 with a 4.22 ERA and 165 strikeouts. He tied Kevin Ritz and Pedro Astacio for the all-time club record in victories.

Francis said shouldering the team's playoff aspirations was more important than the number of games he won. And the bigger the game, the more clutch he became, shutting down the Phillies to get the Rockies playoff run started, then outdueling Webb in Arizona to set the tone for the NLCS sweep.

But it was his work just keeping the Rockies in the race that often got overlooked. As playoff jockeying got more serious, Francis was nails. From June 14 to Aug. 8, he set a franchise record for a starter by winning eight consecutive decisions. But on Aug. 14 at San Diego's Petco Park, the Padres blew Francis off the mound. Lacking essential fastball command, he walked six, gave up six hits and was torched for eight runs in just 3 1/3 innings. It was a case, pitching coach Bob Apodaca said, of Francis trying to pitch too fine.

"It's much like a golfer who's trying to hit a drive and

Lefty Jeff Francis got all the run support he needed in his win Wednesday over the Brewers. *Karl Gehring, The Denver Post*

Jeff Francis shakes hands with manager Clint Hurdle after pitching 2 innings in a preseason game.

Hyoung Chang, The Denver Post

put it into a fairway instead of trusting his swing and just letting it go," Apodaca said. "It's about trusting yourself. It's about Jeff telling himself, 'All my side work and all that film study has prepared me for this, so now I have to trust my talent and just let it go.' It's those little things that are preventing him from the next step."

Francis, a cornerstone of the Rockies' youth movement, signed a four-year, $13.25 million contract last winter. Already the winningest left-hander in Rockies history, he threw 199 innings last season and finished the regular season having thrown 215 1/3 innings.

"I'm always searching for some kind of consistency," Francis said. "I still have points in the season where I have to battle to find things, like my release points, but I think I'm learning that that's what all pitchers go through. You have to learn what to do when you don't have your top stuff."

Francis doesn't throw hard. His fastball usually ranges from 84-88 mph, touching 90 on rare occasions. But that doesn't mean he can't develop into an ace.

"He's not an overpowering pitcher, but players in this game come in different shapes and sizes," Apodaca said. "Tom Glavine won 300 games and has never been accused of being a power pitcher. He's always been somebody who is very workmanlike. I think that's what Jeff can be – very workmanlike."

General manager Dan O'Dowd, who says Francis has grown "tremendously" in his first three seasons in the majors, projects a bright future, in large part because he sees Francis as "a great self-evaluator." ∎

Yorvit Torrealba gave starter Jeff Francis a tap on the chest after the left-hander recorded his 10th strikeout of the game against the Dodgers September 18, 2007. *Karl Gehring, The Denver Post*

A CLOSER LOOK

Young Panamanian Corpas is Rockies' shutdown man-in-waiting

By Patrick Saunders

July 31, 2007

Growing up in a poor neighborhood on the outskirts of Panama City, Manny Corpas was able to watch just two major-league teams on television: the Atlanta Braves and the New York Yankees.

That Yankees reliever Mariano Rivera also hailed from Panama City appealed to Corpas, of course, but there was more to it than that. Corpas found the image of Rivera, staring down opposing batters, then blowing them away, irresistible.

"He was my idol. He motivated me," the Rockies' 24-year-old reliever said.

Corpas took the opportunity to step into pennant-race pressure the likes of which few have mastered as well as Rivera and ran with it after all-star closer Brian Fuentes was sidelined by injury. He was nearly perfect down the stretch to help the Rockies make it to the postseason, then saved five playoff games to help the Rockies make the World Series.

"I think we have all felt that this guy has a special arm," said manager Clint Hurdle.

Saving tight games under pennant pressure is a dream for Corpas, who said it's the role he has wanted to play since he began playing organized baseball at age 14.

"I just like it," he said. "I don't let anything get to me when I'm out there. I just pitch."

He pitched so well that when Fuentes recovered from injury he moved into the setup role and Corpas remained the closer.

"I'm just happy to get an opportunity. It's not something easy, not something that a lot of people can do," Corpas said.

While Corpas possesses a fastball that can hit the high 90s and a wicked slider, his best attribute is his competitiveness. He showed that inner fire in one of his first big tests after taking over for Fuentes. After giving up two singles in the ninth against the Dodgers, he faced Andre Ethier with two outs, the bases full and the Rockies leading 9-6. After an eight-pitch battle, Corpas struck out Ethier on a nasty slider, low and away.

"That's just Manny. He doesn't have any fear," said rookie starter Ubaldo Jimenez, who became friends with Corpas in 2001 when they played baseball together at the Rockies' Latin American training complex in Boca Chica, Dominican Republic.

Corpas' competitive spirit is not his only source of motivation. Escaping poverty has been, too.

"I thank God I was able to play baseball, make some money and get out of there," said Corpas, whose father worked as a laborer in a brewery.

Corpas tried soccer first, but not for long.

"I played one game, but I wasn't very good," he said with a hearty laugh. "They put me in at goalie, and I didn't like that. I told the manager it wasn't for me."

Manny Corpas, catcher Yorvit Torrealba and pitcher Ubaldo Jimenez celebrated their 6-4 victory over the Diamondbacks Monday night to advance to the World Series. *Karl Gehring, The Denver Post*

Manny Corpas has been the stopper for the Colorado Rockies while Brian Fuentes has been injured.

Karl Gehring, The Denver Post

By age 15, Corpas was throwing an 88 mph fastball, playing for Panamanian national teams and signing autographs. The Rockies signed him a year later after seeing him pitch in Taiwan.

"In some ways, there's not much difference to Manny now," said Rolando Fernandez, the Rockies' director of Latin American operations. "He always had good movement on his fastball. He's a quiet guy, but he knows how to go about his business. And he's a guy who was never afraid in any situation."

Fernandez set about honing Corpas' pitching skills, teaching him how to throw a biting slider and stop fooling around with assorted arm angles.

As Corpas grew from a 5-foot-11 beanpole to a 6-3, 195-pound athlete, his fastball kept gaining steam. By the time he was pitching for Single-A Asheville (N.C.) in 2004, his fastball was regularly clocked at 93. He was reaching 98 by the end of his 2005 season at High-A Modesto (Calif.). His whirlwind 2006 season started in Double-A Tulsa, made a pit stop in Triple-A Colorado Springs and finished with the Rockies, where he made 35 appearances with an impressive 3.62 ERA.

Though he struggled on occasion, the Rockies knew then they had uncovered and developed a talented young pitcher.

"I do have to kind of chuckle now," Hurdle said. "I remember when I brought Manny in and he didn't do well, I got a lot of pointed questions about 'How can you bring that young man into this situation?' But I thought he was a special young man then and would have a lot more of those situations in the future." ∎

Manny Corpas

Manny Corpas pitched the final inning against the Diamondbacks helping lead the Colorado Rockies to a win at Coors Field. The win forced a tie-breaking game for the NL wild card.

Helen H. Richardson, The Denver Post

MATSUI EAGER TO BE BIG HIT WITH ROCKIES

By Troy E. Renck

February 20, 2007

Forget Waldo. Where's Kazuo?

The public relations staff members insist they saw him in the batting cage a few days earlier at spring training. Troy Tulowitzki confirms his teammate walked through recently. His interpreter promises that the Rockies second baseman is at Hi Corbett Field.

A few minutes later, an autograph on a fan's baseball card provides a fresh clue. Kazuo Matsui, the international man of mystery, is training alone on a back field. Far removed from prying eyes, Matsui runs laps on the warning track, works on agility drills and does stretches that would make a pretzel cringe.

It is here in the desert, unburdened from the small army of reporters that used to chronicle his every move, where Matsui believes a lost major-league career will be found.

"I had never experienced anything like New York before. I like it here. The Rockies wanted me and I signed back to show my appreciation," Matsui said. "I absolutely believe I can be an (elite) player."

Matsui spoke those words in spring training, then went out and backed them up during a regular season when he hit .288, stole 32 bases and scored 84 runs in 104 games. In the postseason, he was even better. In a first round sweep of the Phillies he was the Rockies best hitter and had the biggest blow, a grand slam off Kyle Lohse that broke Game 2 open.

That Matsui ended up in Colorado has everything to do with New York, a 2 1/2 -year failed experiment that clouds every judgment of the 31-year-old infielder. Is Matsui a star waiting to bloom, the victim of being miscast on the big stage? Or is he just an ordinary player regardless of the uniform?

After Matsui batted .345 in 32 games with them last year, the Rockies made retaining the switch hitter a priority, quickly signing him to a $1.5 million contract – a shadow of his $20 million deal with the Mets. Matsui settled in at the No. 2 spot behind Willy Taveras to help set the table for the National League's second most productive offense.

"We want him to be in control of the game. If he's not running, he's not using all of his tools," new baserunning and outfield coach Glenallen Hill said in the spring. "And we want him to know that it's OK to make a mistake."

That statement provided a hint of how Matsui's career careened off the tracks in New York. He is a perfectionist, an admirable quality that ate his

Kaz Matsui makes a play on a ball hit up the middle. *Karl Gehring, The Denver Post*

insides when he failed to make a smooth transition to the big leagues.

Former Mets general manager Steve Phillips didn't sign Matsui, but was in charge as the organization built the scouting reports that led to his big contract.

"Those reports were unbelievable. They indicated that he was a Robbie Alomar type, but a shortstop," Phillips said. "He didn't handle New York well, then he got uptight and it only got worse."

Phillips believes Colorado is a perfect stage for Matsui's comeback, saying "he's that rare veteran with an upside. If he regains his confidence, his talent will play out."

Even before Matsui shared a laugh with Todd Helton in the parking lot during a lazy spring training morning, it was clear he is more comfortable with the Rockies. Denver, he said, reminds him of Tokorozawa, the hilly countryside city where he

Kazuo Matsui greets a contingent of Japanese media during batting practice. *John Leyba, The Denver Post*

starred for the Seibu Lions. Talk of him returning to the Japanese League this winter was off base, he confirmed.

His pride stung, he wasn't about to give up on his big-league dreams.

"I wasn't healthy in New York and didn't play well. I came here to be successful," Matsui said. "I didn't want to go back like that."

He also saw the ball better this season after trying unsuccessfully to wear contact lens.

"He had problems with his eyes in New York," Mets coach Sandy Alomar Sr. said. "He makes no excuses and works hard. Denver will be good for him. He holds a lot of things inside, you just have to talk to him." ∎

Kazuo Matsui and teammates celebrate their 2-1 victory after Manny Corpas got the last out and a sweep of Game 3 of the NLDS. *John Leyba, The Denver Post*

LATINO TRIO ADD FINAL ZING

The Rockies wouldn't be where they are without the unexpected emergence of Jimenez, Corpas and Morales
By Troy E. Renck

October 14, 2007

On a quiet morning in March two years ago, Rockies general manager Dan O'Dowd identified a factor that could help his team come of age.

"We need to find our Bartolo Colon," O'Dowd said of the standout Dominican pitcher as he walked to a practice field in Tucson.

For the Rockies' first seven years, the idea of injecting talent through Latin America was an afterthought. They paid lip service, but little money. Not surprisingly, they received little help from those countries, shortstop Neifi Perez being the lone high-profile player.

The impact the Rockies have thirsted for, and in truth, desperately needed, arrived not with a drip but a tidal wave this season. As the Rockies prepare to host their first-ever NL Championship Series game at Coors Field tonight, they owe a huge debt to three young pitchers, Dominican Ubaldo Jimenez, Panamanian Manny Corpas and Venezuelan Franklin Morales.

"We wouldn't be here without those three," pitching coach Bob Apodaca said. "There's no way around it."

In any improbable story, there are moments when logic takes a sabbatical. Everything can't make sense or there wouldn't be movies made about the 1980 U.S. Olympic hockey team or kids named after the 1969 Miracle Mets. So it is with the Rockies and their trio of power arms.

If the Rockies wanted to paint themselves as the smartest person in the room, they would insist the troika's arrival was planned. Not exactly.

"Just getting that flow of talent into our system and the impact it has made, it is huge," O'Dowd said. "But it came out of necessity more than anything else."

With Jimenez and Morales, injuries created opportunities in the starting rotation in July and August. Manny Corpas took over when all-star closer Brian Fuentes blew four consecutive saves, then went onto the disabled list.

It's impossible to overstate their contribution. The Rockies have won 11 consecutive games started by Jimenez and Morales, including NLCS Game 2 on Friday night when Jimenez allowed just one run in five innings.

Morales, 21, started Game 4, just three months

Franklin Morales pitches in Game 1 of the World Series between the Colorado Rockies and the Boston Red Sox at Fenway Park. *Andy Cross, The Denver Post*

Ubaldo Jimenez stands in the shadows of the bullpen at Chase Field. *RJ Sangosti, The Denver Post*

removed from Double-A baseball. Corpas has failed only twice in save opportunities, and even those failures came with an asterisk. He limited the damage by San Diego on Sept. 21 and Arizona on Friday, keeping the game tied. In both cases the Rockies won in extra innings.

"It's great to see what we have done," Jimenez said. "It's not something we expected."

The man responsible, in many ways, for adding this rocket fuel to the Rockies' ride is Rolando Fernandez, director of Latin operations, and his scouts. One of O'Dowd's first moves back in 1999 was to promote Fernandez, recognizing "that he was special and needed a bigger role."

Fernandez's project was daunting, digging for talent with a pickax. But the Rockies pumped more money into his scouting budget and he made shrewd decisions, signing Morales at 16 and Jimenez and Corpas at 17 for approximately $100,000 combined.

For a franchise that was thrown upside down financially after the aborted Mike Hampton and Denny Neagle contracts, that amounted to hitting the lottery with an investment.

"Everybody from the scouts to myself to O'Dowd, to (assistant GM) Bill Geivett and (scouting director) Bill Schmidt can't stop talking about how proud we are of these guys," explained Fernandez, who had the final say when signing the three pitchers. "I definitely believed in them, but they are performing great sooner than I expected."

Fernandez is not a detached observer. He remains close to his players long after they leave the Latin American academies. He had an idea that Jimenez would pop in the big leagues because he was trying too hard in the minor leagues. That Jimenez is a

Ubaldo Jimenez in Game 2 of the World Series between the Colorado Rockies and the Boston Red Sox.

John Leyba, The Denver Post

Manny Corpas comes in to close out the game as the Colorado Rockies defeat the Phillies. *John Leyba, The Denver Post*

Rockie is an example of how small concessions can make a big picture come into focus. He's in a Colorado uniform today because of school. He grew up, in his words, "in the 'hood."

Baseball was his dream, but his vision was broader than the diamond.

"They offered me more money, $40,000 to sign," Jimenez said. "But they were the only ones that let me finish school. I wanted my high school (diploma). And they helped me get that. It meant a lot."

Both throw hard with such incredible movement – "I would be shocked if Jimenez doesn't get a no-hitter in his career," admitted Rockies third baseman Garrett Atkins – that hitters would rather chew tinfoil than face them.

"They are uncomfortable. You're talking about elite power arms," said San Diego GM Kevin Towers.

Corpas, 24, is just about as nasty, his career accelerated by a stint in the Venezuelan winter league a few years ago. Setup man LaTroy Hawkins refers to

the kid's stuff as electric. And his personality suits his role as he remains cool, unbothered by the magnitude of his job.

"We thought he could handle it, but really until a guy does it in the ninth inning, you don't know," Apodaca said. "He doesn't fear contact. And he goes right after the hitters. Nothing bothers him."

Well, almost nothing. According to Hawkins, Corpas always has an eye peeled and an ear raised when the other Latino guys start razzing him. It is a tight group.

So, as the Rockies earned a World Series berth, this threesome stands tall, a huge figure in Colorado's rise from the ashes.

"No words can put in perspective how important they have been for us this season," O'Dowd said. "And how important they will be in the future." ■

Corpas became the stopper for the Rockies after Brian Fuentes went down with an injury. *Karl Gehring, The Denver Post*

SECRET TO SUCCESS IS SIMPLE

By Woody Paige Denver Post Staff Columnist

October 11, 2007

In sports, bandwagon effect is a term for people who begin flocking to a team after they have achieved success. – Wikipedia

Please make room on the back of the bandwagon for an old, red-faced clown who plays the calliope.

Phweep, phweep, boomp, boomp, boomp, phweep, phweep, boomp, phweep. This gorgeous wagon of The Sells-Floto Circus & Buffalo Bill's Wild West Show (owned by The Denver Post) – built in 1916, 10 feet high and 24 feet long, painted bright purple, with gold inlay swirls and wood carvings of lions, tigers, elephants, Padres, Phillies and snakes – and is listing to the right.

We're gonna need a bigger wagon.

It won't hold 4 million bandwagon-jumpers.

In 1848, renowned circus clown Dan Rice invited presidential candidate Zachary Taylor to ride on his bandwagon at appearances around the country. As Taylor became admired and accepted, more and more politicians, who had been skeptical, asked to hop onto the bandwagon. Today, so many people say that they knew from the very beginning that the Rockies would be right here where they are.

To that, I play: Phweep, boomp.

Truth is, few people believed in the Rockies, and the vast majority, including me (prominently), did-n't believe.

A three-game Rockies-Diamondbacks series in mid-May drew an announced average of 21,237 (although the actual number was much lower) to Coors Field. The Rockies lost two of three and fell to 17-25. Not much to believe in then.

This week I asked a straightforward baseball Dalai Lama, so close to the Rockies he can touch them – and he's not in the media or a scout, and he wasn't driving the bandwagon early – how they did it.

"They all just started playing well at the same time."

That's the secret of life, maharishi?

"(Garrett) Atkins was struggling for a long time, but he burst out. Brad Hawpe went through a slump, then came out of it. Todd Helton was in a funk for a while, but look what he did at the end of the season. After the all-star break (Kazuo) Matsui couldn't hit a lick, and got hurt, but he was the MVP of the Phillies series. Tulo (Troy Tulowitzki) got better and better at the bat as the season went along. (Yorvit) Torrealba and Chris Iannetta split behind the plate, and neither was hitting much. When Iannetta was sent down and Torrealba played every day, he got confident with the bat. When Iannetta came back, he found his bat.

"Jamey Carroll came through with some big hits, including the flyball in the play-in game. Jeff Baker

returned from the DL, then got the pinch-hit single to win the last game with the Phillies. When (Willy) Taveras got hurt, Cory Sullivan and Ryan Spilborghs picked up the Rockies in center. Remember, they dropped John Mabry and Steve Finley, who were finished as hitters. Seth Smith and Ian Stewart contributed.

"And Matt Holliday was the only player there every day all season.

"So, when the streak (17-of-18) started, all of them started hitting."

What about the pitching, guru?

"Same thing. They all started pitching great at the same time.

"Their closer (Brian Fuentes) labored and blew some saves, then was put onto the DL. When he came back from the back problem, he was the perfect setup man. They were forced to use (Manny) Corpas as the closer, and he came through like a champ. Matt

Herges, he was outstanding down the stretch. The rest of the bullpen was steady and often spectacular.

"They lose three starting pitchers and find two great young pitchers who have pitched beyond belief. Those two F's (Jeff Francis and Josh Fogg) did the job over and over, and they got through the fifth spot with duct tape and Saran Wrap and Mark Redman.

"It's amazing how every move Clint Hurdle made was the right one. In Philadelphia he didn't do anything that would come back to bite him in the butt.

"They were the little engine that could. They thought they could, then they knew they could. Who else knew?" the wise one said.

The world's largest bandwagon (4 million people and one calliope-playing clown) and the Rockies roll on to the World Series.

Rox in six.

Phweep, phweep, boomp, boomp, phweep, boomp. ■

A Magical Season

DATE	OPPONENT	SCORE	PLACE	THE SKINNY
4/2/07	Arizona	L 6-8	t-3rd	Rox rough up Brandon Webb, but LaTroy Hawkins cannot hold it in the pen
4/3/07	Arizona	W 4-3x	t-2nd	Troy Tulowitzki doubles and scores in the 11th
4/4/07	Arizona	W 11-4	2nd	Rodrigo Lopez shines in Rox debut, Matt Holliday-led offense stomps D-backs
4/6/07	at San Diego	W 4-3	1st	Rox outlast the Padres and take 1st place
4/7/07	at San Diego	L 2-3	t-2nd	Manny Corpas loses to Trevor Hoffman in the 9th, Rockies drop from 1st
4/8/07	at San Diego	L 1-2x	4th	San Diego wins in 10, Jake Peavy and Padres pen shuts down Colorado
4/9/07	at LA Dodgers	W 6-3	t-3rd	Jeff Francis gets his first win of the year, Garrett Atkins: 3 RBI
4/10/07	at LA Dodgers	L 1-2	4th	Rox offense AWOL in late-inning loss
4/11/07	at LA Dodgers	L 0-3	4th	Brad Penny and Co. two-hit the scoreless Rox
4/13/07	at Arizona	W 6-3	4th	Todd Helton drives in 2
4/14/07	at Arizona	L 4-5	4th	D-backs seal the deal in the 8th, Hawkins stumbles to 3rd loss
4/15/07	at Arizona	L 4-6	4th	Homerin' Helton not enough to overcome Tony Clark and the D-backs
4/16/07	San Francisco	L 0-8	4th	Barry Zito shackles Rox, Giants flog Francis for 7 runs
4/17/07	San Francisco	W 5-3	4th	Yorvit Torrealba doubles in 3, 5-run 8th beats San Francisco
4/18/07	LA Dodgers	W 7-2	4th	Holliday: 3-for-4 with 2 runs scored, Torrealba and Tulo each drive in 2
4/19/07	LA Dodgers	L 1-8	4th	Derailed Rox offense succumbs to balanced Dodgers attack
4/20/07	San Diego	L 1-11	5th	Josh Fogg pummeled for 7
4/21/07	San Diego	L 3-7	5th	Brian Giles' 4 hits foil Francis
4/22/07	San Diego	W 4-2	5th	Holliday goes 3-for-4 in win over Greg Maddux and the Padres
4/23/07	at NY Mets	L 1-6	5th	Helton and Holliday combined 5 for 7 at the plate in Rox loss
4/24/07	at NY Mets	L 1-2x	5th	Rox pen sours in the Big Apple despite Tulo's 10th-inning heroics
4/25/07	at NY Mets	W 11-5	5th	Shea faithful silenced, Taveras breaks out of slump going 5-6
4/27/07	Atlanta	L 7-9	5th	9th-inning rally dies when Holliday's potential game-tier is caught
4/28/07	Atlanta	L 2-6	5th	Tulo's first-inning homer cannot topple John Smoltz and the Braves
4/29/07	Atlanta	W 9-7x	5th	Tulo's unassisted triple play in the 7th, Holliday 2-run homer in the 11th
4/30/07	at San Francisco	L 5-9	5th	Tulo 4-for-4 but offense strands 9 in defeat
5/1/07	at San Francisco	W 9-7	5th	Alberto Arias wins in major-league debut, Holliday homers and drives in 4
5/2/07	at San Francisco	L 3-5	5th	Barry Bonds homers and knocks in 4 as San Fran rally knocks off Rox
5/4/07	at Cincinnati	W 6-5x	5th	Helton homers early and Tulo wins it in the 11th with RBI single
5/5/07	at Cincinnati	W 9-7	5th	Holliday and Chris Iannetta homer, Rox take first series since opener
5/6/07	at Cincinnati	L 3-9	5th	Fogg coughs up 5 earned runs
5/7/07	at St. Louis	W 3-2	5th	Brad Hawpe's 9th-inning, bases-loaded walk wins it for Rox
5/8/07	at St. Louis	L 1-4	5th	Bullpen implodes in 7th to spoil Holliday's 3-for-4 evening
5/9/07	at St. Louis	L 2-9	5th	Defending champs school Rox with relentless attack
5/10/07	San Francisco	W 5-3	5th	Aaron Cook's sacrifice bunts and Tulo's 2 RBI key victory
5/11/07	San Francisco	L 3-8	5th	Fogg no-hits Giants into 6th before surrendering the winning runs
5/12/07	San Francisco	W 6-2	5th	Francis sharp, Holliday goes deep -- twice -- in win
5/13/07	San Francisco	L 2-15	5th	SF rookie Fred Lewis hits for the cycle as Giants blow out the Rox
5/15/07	Arizona	L 0-3	5th	Randy Johnson tosses 6 shutout innings as Rox go quietly
5/16/07	Arizona	W 5-3	5th	Brad Hawpe homers twice, Cook effective in win over D-backs

Stats

DATE	OPPONENT	SCORE	PLACE	THE SKINNY
5/17/07	Arizona	L 1-3	5th	Fogg takes tough loss against Livan Hernandez
5/18/07	Kansas City	L 2-5	5th	Royals top Rox with 5-run 8th
5/19/07	Kansas City	W 6-4	5th	Atkins gets his groove back on 3-run homer, Helton and Hawpe also homer
5/20/07	Kansas City	L 5-10x	5th	KC scores 5 times in 12th to crush Rox comeback
5/21/07	at Arizona	L 5-6	5th	Kaz Matsui's 3 RBI and Hawpe's homer come up short in Phoenix
5/22/07	at Arizona	W 3-1	5th	Rox notch win with Tulo's 9th-inning RBI double
5/23/07	at Arizona	W 2-0	5th	Ryan Spilborghs offensive as dominant Francis dispatches D-backs
5/25/07	at San Francisco	W 5-3	5th	Matsui knocks in 9th inning go-ahead run, Holliday goes 3-for-5
5/26/07	at San Francisco	W 6-1	5th	The good times roll behind Cook's complete game and Holliday's 3 RBI
5/27/07	at San Francisco	W 6-4x	5th	Tulo and Iannetta provide 10th inning pop, Helton 4-for-5
5/28/07	St. Louis	W 6-2	5th	Francis locks down the Cards and Holliday homers
5/29/07	St. Louis	W 8-3	4th	Rox win streak climbs to 7 behind Torrealba's homer and 4 RBI
5/30/07	St. Louis	L 4-8	5th	Pujols-powered Cards snap Rox streak at 7, Holliday homers
5/31/07	St. Louis	L 3-7	5th	Hawpe goes 2-for-4 in losing effort against banged up St. Louis
6/1/07	Cincinnati	L 2-4	5th	Willy Taveras 3-for-5, Helton 2-for-5 in loss to the Reds
6/2/07	Cincinnati	W 4-1	5th	Francis: 5 hits over 7 innings, Helton goes deep
6/3/07	Cincinnati	W 10-9x	4th	Matsui leads the charge in come from behind slugfest
6/5/07	Houston	L 1-4	5th	Lance Berkman drives in 2 as Houston dismantles Rox
6/6/07	Houston	W 8-7	4th	Hawpe and Matsui chip in 2 RBI apiece in Rox win
6/7/07	Houston	W 7-6	4th	Tulo's 2-run homer starts comeback, RBI single in the 9th caps win
6/8/07	at Baltimore	L 2-4	4th	Both managers ejected as O's roll over Rockies
6/9/07	at Baltimore	W 3-2x	4th	Late inning Rox worth staying up for - Matsui doubles in winning run
6/10/07	at Baltimore	W 6-1	4th	Spilborghs: 2 homers, 6 RBI; Jason Hirsh pitches complete game
6/12/07	at Boston	L 1-2	4th	Rox knuckle under Tim Wakefield's soft serve
6/13/07	at Boston	W 12-2	4th	Rox knock Sox for 12, Hawpe homers, 3 RBI, Helton drives in 4
6/14/07	at Boston	W 7-1	4th	Atkins hits grand slam over the Monster, Josh Beckett suffers first loss
6/15/07	Tampa Bay	W 12-2	4th	Atkins and Hawpe smack back-to-back homers
6/16/07	Tampa Bay	W 10-5	4th	Taveras, Atkins and Hawpe homer in romp over Tampa.
6/17/07	Tampa Bay	L 4-7	4th	Tampa Bay cools hot Rox on strength of Carlos Pena's moonshot
6/19/07	NY Yankees	W 3-1	4th	Torrealba goes yard, Fogg fends off Yanks at Coors
6/20/07	NY Yankees	W 6-1	4th	Yanks can't solve Francis, Holliday homers and knocks in 3
6/21/07	NY Yankees	W 4-3	4th	Bronx boom goes bust, Tulo, Atkins and Matsui homer, sweep Yanks
6/22/07	at Toronto	L 8-9x	4th	Tulo's 2-run, 10th-inning homer erased as Jays rally for 3 in bottom of 10th
6/23/07	at Toronto	L 6-11	4th	Matt Stairs and Frank Thomas put the big hurt on Cook
6/24/07	at Toronto	L 0-5	4th	Dustin McGowan nearly no-hits hapless Rox
6/25/07	at Chi. Cubs	L 9-10	4th	6-run 9th not enough to stop Cub walk off win
6/26/07	at Chi. Cubs	L 5-8	4th	Cubs break out early and hold of Rox in the 9th
6/27/07	at Chi. Cubs	L 4-6	4th	Rox swept for second straight series, woeful at Wrigley
6/28/07	at Houston	L 5-8x	4th	Craig Biggio gets 3,000th hit, Carlos Lee's 11th-inning grand slam dooms Rox
6/29/07	at Houston	L 8-9	4th	Brian Fuentes blows 4th save in 8 days, losing skid at 8

A Magical Season

DATE	OPPONENT	SCORE	PLACE	THE SKINNY
6/30/07	at Houston	W 5-0	4th	Francis beats Jason Jennings, losing streak snapped
7/1/07	at Houston	L 0-12	4th	Houston manhandles Colorado
7/2/07	NY Mets	W 6-2	4th	Rox resume winning ways, Holliday: 3-run homer
7/3/07	NY Mets	W 11-3	4th	Matsui's five hits and Spilborghs' slam fuel Rox rout of Mets
7/4/07	NY Mets	W 17-7	4th	Rox sweep Mets on 20 hits, 5 RBI from Helton and Atkins
7/6/07	Philadelphia	W 7-6x	4th	Helton flashes glove in 11th to set up Torrealba's game-winning hit
7/7/07	Philadelphia	W 6-3	4th	Manny Corpas notches 1st save as win streak hits 5
7/8/07	Philadelphia	L 4-8	4th	Phils save grounds crew from runaway tarp, run away with victory
7/13/07	at Milwaukee	W 10-6	4th	Tulo and Torrealba rip 2-run homers in the fifth
7/14/07	at Milwaukee	L 1-2x	4th	With the infield in, time runs out on Rox in 10th
7/15/07	at Milwaukee	L 3-4	4th	Jeremy Affeldt's wild pitch tips scale in favor of Milwaukee
7/16/07	at Pittsburgh	W 10-8	4th	Rockies nearly cough up early 9-1 lead but pen prevails
7/17/07	at Pittsburgh	W 6-2	4th	Fogg fells former team, Rox win their first series at PNC Park
7/18/07	at Pittsburgh	W 5-3	4th	Francis wins 5th straight, Hawpe and Helton hit 2-run homers
7/19/07	at Washington	L 4-5x	4th	Nats pass Rox in 10, Tulo and Atkins homer
7/20/07	at Washington	W 3-1	t-3rd	Cook fans 8 while Rox do the little things to win
7/21/07	at Washington	L 0-3	4th	Nats pitchers hold Rox to just one hit after the 1st
7/22/07	at Washington	L 0-3	4th	Rox strand 10 in second consecutive shutout
7/23/07	San Diego	W 7-5	4th	Holliday and Hawpe homer in 8th as Rox rough up Pads pen
7/24/07	San Diego	L 3-5	4th	Late-inning surge falls flat in San Diego
7/25/07	San Diego	W 10-2	4th	Cook tosses 74-pitch complete game
7/26/07	LA Dodgers	L 4-5	4th	Hawpe's 3 RBI not enough as Dodgers win by 1
7/28/07	LA Dodgers	W 6-2	4th	Francis wins 6th in a row
7/29/07	LA Dodgers	W 9-6	4th	Ubaldo Jimenez's first major-league victory, Holliday knocks in 3
7/31/07	at Florida	W 6-3	4th	Cook effective, Holliday 3 for 4, Atkins 3 RBI
8/1/07	at Florida	L 3-4	4th	Byung-Hyun Kim fans 10 Rox, late rally falls short
8/2/07	at Florida	W 4-3	4th	Holliday doubles and scores in 8th-inning rally
8/3/07	at Atlanta	W 9-2	4th	Atkins: 3-run homer, Francis wins 7th straight
8/4/07	at Atlanta	L 4-6	4th	Tim Hudson holds Rox scoreless through 7, Atkins' grand slam in vain
8/5/07	at Atlanta	L 5-6x	4th	Yunel Escobar spells extra-inning heartbreak
8/6/07	Milwaukee	W 6-2	4th	Helton, Hawpe pounce on Brewers early, Holliday homers
8/7/07	Milwaukee	W 11-4	t-3rd	Helton homers twice, drives in 4
8/8/07	Milwaukee	W 19-4	3rd	Rox sweep Brewers, Atkins: 6 RBI, Spilborghs, Hawpe and Tulo go deep
8/9/07	Chi. Cubs	L 2-10	t-3rd	Cubs' 5-run 3rd undoes Rox
8/10/07	Chi. Cubs	L 2-6	4th	Tulo drives in 2 but Rox lose
8/11/07	Chi. Cubs	W 15-2	t-3rd	Jamey Carroll's pinch-hit grand slam breaks open tie game in 6th
8/12/07	Chi. Cubs	W 6-3	3rd	Tulo homers, doubles in go-ahead run to collect 3 RBI
8/14/07	at San Diego	L 0-8	3rd	Francis shelled as Rox bats take day off
8/15/07	at San Diego	W 3-0	3rd	Jimenez picks up team, Ian Stewart knocks in 2
8/16/07	at San Diego	L 9-11	3rd	San Diego's 9-run inning too much to overcome
8/17/07	at LA Dodgers	L 4-6	4th	Rox strike out 12 times in loss
8/18/07	at LA Dodgers	W 7-4x	3rd	Holliday and Cory Sullivan spearhead 3-run rally in 14th

Stats

DATE	OPPONENT	SCORE	PLACE	THE SKINNY
8/19/07	at LA Dodgers	L 3-4	4th	Ramon Martinez knocks in 3 as Dodgers rally in 8th
8/20/07	Pittsburgh	L 2-4x	4th	Rox fail to hold 8th-inning lead for third consecutive game
8/21/07	Pittsburgh	W 9-2	t-3rd	Stewart grand slam, Tulowitzki, Holliday and Hawpe also homer
8/22/07	Pittsburgh	L 2-11	4th	Pittsburgh socks 6 homers in rout
8/23/07	Pittsburgh	L 1-5	4th	Rox muster one run as Pirates take series
8/24/07	Washington	W 6-5	4th	Holliday's 2-run homer in 9th triggers 5 run rally
8/25/07	Washington	W 5-1	t-3rd	Stingy Jimenez allows 3 hits over 7 innings
8/26/07	Washington	W 10-5	t-3rd	Holliday: 1 homer, 3RBI, Helton: 3-for-4, Tulo: 3 RBI
8/27/07	at San Francisco	L 1-4	4th	Jorge Julio implodes, allows 3 runs in the 8th
8/28/07	at San Francisco	L 1-3	4th	Matt Cain keeps Rox in check
8/29/07	at San Francisco	W 8-0	4th	Francis tosses shutout as Atkins homers twice and knocks in 4
8/31/07	at Arizona	W 7-3x	4th	Rox rally late, pen shuts down D-backs in extra innings
9/1/07	at Arizona	L 7-13	4th	Tony Clark's 5 RBI pace D-backs
9/2/07	at Arizona	W 4-3	4th	Tulo's heads-up defense catches Justin Upton off third
9/3/07	San Francisco	W 7-4	4th	Francis doubles and scores, gets win
9/4/07	San Francisco	W 6-5	4th	Hawpe's single wins it in 9th
9/5/07	San Francisco	L 3-5	4th	Giants avoid sweep, Barry Bonds goes deep
9/7/07	San Diego	W 10-4	4th	Rox use 10 pitchers, break game open in 8th
9/8/07	San Diego	L 1-3	4th	Greg Maddux stymies Colorado
9/9/07	San Diego	W 4-2	4th	Rox win on just 4 hits, Atkins and Holliday homer
9/10/07	at Philadelphia	L 5-6x	4th	Ryan Howard doubles in game winner in 10th
9/11/07	at Philadelphia	W 8-2	t-3rd	Franklin Morales pitches 5 scoreless innings, Holliday homers twice
9/12/07	at Philadelphia	W 12-0	t-3rd	Holliday lines into triple play, atones in next at-bat with 3-run homer
9/13/07	at Philadelphia	L 4-12	4th	Phils tag Francis for 8 runs
9/14/07	Florida	L 6-7	4th	Dontrelle Willis and Marlins pen hold off Rox
9/15/07	Florida	L 2-10	4th	Rox drop third straight as Marlins romp
9/16/07	Florida	W 13-0	4th	Helton pounds 300th homer, Rox return to win column
9/18/07	LA Dodgers	W 3-1	4th	Francis strikes out 10
9/18/07	LA Dodgers	W -9-8	t-3rd	Helton's 9th-inning homer dogs Dodgers -- win streak at 3
9/19/07	LA Dodgers	W 6-5	3rd	Hawpe's 8th-inning homer dispatches LA
9/20/07	LA Dodgers	W 9-4	3rd	Holliday and Tulo homer, sweep Dodgers
9/21/07	at San Diego	W 2-1x	3rd	Hawpe provides pop: game-winning homer in 14th
9/22/07	at San Diego	W 6-2	3rd	Rox run streak to seven, Hawpe: 2 RBI
9/23/07	at San Diego	W 7-3	3rd	Francis tops Maddux, sweep Padres
9/25/07	at LA Dodgers	W 9-7	3rd	Rox eliminate Dodgers, Tulo homers, Helton drives in 2
9/26/07	at LA Dodgers	W 2-0	3rd	Fogg & pen run streak to 10
9/27/07	at LA Dodgers	W 10-4	3rd	Rox turn it up to 11, franchise record streak continues
9/28/07	Arizona	L 2-4	3rd	Brandon Webb beats Francis, D-backs clinch postseason berth at Coors
9/29/07	Arizona	W 11-1	3rd	Raucous Rox remain in hunt, Tulo knocks grand slam
9/30/07	Arizona	W 4-3	t-2nd	Jimenez stellar, pen outlasts D-backs as Rox survive
10/1/07	San Diego	W 9-8x	2nd	Matsui + Tulo + Holliday + Carroll = Wild Card in 13th!

Compiled by Barry Osborne of the Denver Post Research Library